Remote Work

The First Step to Running Your Own Business

© Copyright 2019 by
_____ -
All rights reserved.

This content is provided with the sole purpose of providing relevant information on a specific topic for which every reasonable effort has been made to ensure that it is both accurate and reasonable. Nevertheless, by purchasing this content you consent to the fact that the author, as well as the publisher, are in no way experts on the topics contained herein, regardless of any claims as such that may be made within. As such, any suggestions or recommendations that are made within are done so purely for entertainment value. It is recommended that you always consult a professional prior to undertaking any of the advice or techniques discussed within.

This is a legally binding declaration that is considered both valid and fair by both the Committee of Publishers

Association and the American Bar Association and should be considered as legally binding within the United States.

The reproduction, transmission, and duplication of any of the content found herein, including any specific or extended information will be done as an illegal act regardless of the end form the information ultimately takes. This includes copied versions of the work both physical, digital and audio unless express consent of the Publisher is provided beforehand. Any additional rights reserved.

Furthermore, the information that can be found within the pages described forthwith shall be considered both accurate and truthful when it comes to the recounting of facts. As such, any use, correct or incorrect, of the provided information will render the Publisher free of responsibility as to the actions taken outside of their direct purview. Regardless, there are zero scenarios where the original author or the Publisher can be deemed liable in any fashion for any damages or hardships that may result from any of the information discussed herein.

Additionally, the information in the following pages is intended only for informational purposes and should thus be thought of as universal. As befitting its nature, it is presented without assurance regarding its prolonged validity or interim quality. Trademarks that are mentioned are done without written consent and can in no way be considered an endorsement from the trademark holder.

Table of Contents

Remote Work
Introduction
Section 1
Chapter 1: Why Remote Work Is the First Step to Running Your Own Business
Chapter 2: What Type of Remote Jobs Are Available
Chapter 3: How to Get Your First Remote Jobs
Section 2
Chapter 4: Time Management
Chapter 5: Teamwork and Communication
Chapter 6: Remote Work and Starting a Business
Conclusion
Description

Introduction

Congratulations on downloading *Remote Work* and thank you for doing so.

The following chapters will discuss the reasons why you should quit your full time job and start working remotely leading to you setting up an entrepreneurial venture. The first chapter identifies the benefits of entrepreneurship and working remotely as compared to holding down an office job. In the following chapter, there is an invigorative discussion of the different types of remote jobs available for anybody to begin. In the third chapter, there is a discussion of how to get your first remote job and the steps you have to follow to ensure success. The forth chapter provides information about how to manage time effectively to ensure that you maximize your opportunities while at work and starting an entrepreneurial enterprise. The fifth chapter identifies the essence of good team work and communication among remote workers to maximize income and yields. The final chapter provides a discussion of the ways of starting your entrepreneurship while avoiding common pitfalls and scams. There is a lot of comprehensive information on the measures that businesses can take to encourage other entrepreneurs to start venturing into this profitable field. The book also contains advice on the best business practices for beginners that will ensure their companies achieve initial success.

There are plenty of books on this subject on the market, thanks again for choosing this one! Every effort was made to ensure it is full of as much useful information as possible, please enjoy!

Section 1
Chapter 1: Why Remote Work Is the First Step to Entrepreneurship

Are you in a traditional job?

Do you have to report to an office every day? Work very closely under the supervision of your boss, and even being in a dead end job at leaves you extremely exhausted at the end of the day? Then you should consider working remotely.

In the white-collar industry, remote jobs have long been viewed as freelance positions that do not generate enough money and cannot support living standards just like a traditional job. Most people have never even considered working from home because they see it as a lazy way of avoiding real work.

Remote jobs have actually become increasingly popular with

the younger generations in society. Older generations have far held the belief that working in offices under an employer is the direct way of earning a living.

Most people have viewed remote jobs with a lot of resentment, claiming that it is just another way of retiring. However, the simple fact remains that remote jobs have not only become popular in the modern world but the most straightforward way of making money in today's business climate.

The emergence of large corporations throughout the twentieth century has encouraged several people to get jobs working for a recognizable organization. Employment has been seen as the key method of achieving progress in life and satisfying most ambitions.

But there are several benefits of working remotely that completely replaces the need for people to work in offices. In fact, in today's world, only a very small percentage of the working force should have a viable reason to be reporting to an office on a daily basis.

Most jobs that are emerging require the workers to work in a flexible manner. There is no need to report to work as long as you can guarantee a certain work yield that allows the organization to progress. Similarly, most remote jobs are based on results rather than employees showing up to a work station.

Despite the obvious advantages of remote jobs, there are some disadvantages that have also to be considered. It is wise for each individual to make a routine that works for them because not everybody's schedule can be the same.

Remote work sometimes requires the freelancer to be up at odd hours of the night, but it is also possible to work during normal working hours just like anybody else who has to report to an office. Either way, having a full comprehension of what is involved in terms of remote work is absolutely important in ensuring success.

Most people also acknowledge that starting remote work marks the beginning of entrepreneurship. At least even people in employment can admit that starting their own business is just as important as the ob they have.

Having your own business means that you are your own boss. You have very little restrictions and everything is hinged on the actual work you put in to your enterprise. Even people in employment would not mind giving up their jobs if it meant that they have a chance of working closely in their own enterprise.

When you start working remotely, you start taking the first steps into entrepreneurship.

If your work is profitable and can grow, you will soon be hiring other people to work for you to maintain the growth of your enterprise.

Starting a business usually is the first step to setting yourself free and working for yourself. People who have their own businesses usually let their money work for them rather than constantly working for money.

You should make the decision to do work remotely is a sustainable manner depending on your own ambitions and plans for your future. You will soon discover that remote work is just as rewarding as employment, and to some level, it is even more beneficial.

It is necessary to understand the various benefits and reasons for doing remote work as opposed to constantly reporting to an office. First, remote work has the advantage of drastically reducing overhead costs both for the employees and the employer.

This is an advantage that works both ways because employees do not have to incur normal daily costs of reporting to an office, such as buying themselves lunch every day. If you are working from home, you reduce so many obligations in terms of what you would normally spend on a normal day.

There are a lot of expenses somebody incurs the moment they step out of their front door. However, if you reduce these expenses by simply not leaving the house but still being productive, then you have a chance of boosting your income.

As for employers, it is best for them to avoid having an office because they get rid of multiple large expenses, such as rent and employee overhead expenses. Working from home eliminates such a multitude of expenses that will result in the fortunes of the enterprise increasing almost overnight.

The simple truth is that office space has become too expensive in the modern world today. Also, there are several workers out there willing to work from home, and this eliminates such large expenses, allowing both the employer and employee to benefit at the same time.

The reduction of costs works in everybody's favor an also allows the employees to work n freedom and comfort that they might not otherwise enjoy in the office. Thus, remote work is a direct contributor to increasing profits in your organization by eliminating several expenses.

Remote work is the first step to entrepreneurship because it will allow you to learn crucial time management skills. There is nothing more important than controlling the amount of time you have in the most productive way so as to boost your yields.

When you start working remotely, you immediately realize that setting deadlines and meeting them is entirely up to you. It is upon you to select a reasonable amount of work that you can complete within a definite time frame to ensure the success of your enterprise.

Therefore, most remote workers are forced to learn crucial time management skills that enable them to maximize on the profitability of their business by keeping operations going. While offices have definite closing hours as well as working hours for the rest of the working population, it can be difficult to get anything done after-hours.

However, with remote work, it does not matter whether it is noon time or midnight, it is still possible to get work done and completed. Time management enables a larger amount of work to be completed as compared to working within definite office hours that have no guarantee of work success.

Most people underestimate the importance of managing time. Imagine being able to complete the amount of work you usually do in your office every week within a couple of days. This will allow you to increase your income and increase your daily turnover.

This is one of the crucial advantages of working remotely as time management becomes an art rather than a rule to follow. You will start taking notice of how you spend your time, and you will be able to organize your own personal time to ensure that you are constantly working and improving your yields.

It is important to note that most remote workers get paid based on their work output. While some might see this as a disadvantage because you will have to be doing a certain amount of work to completion to be paid, others see this as a massive advantage.

Being paid on the basis of results can be very lucrative because your own work yield will determine how much you can earn. If you are a hard worker and have few other obligations, you can focus a large part of your time on your remote job to devastating success.

Working based on your own results is particularly motivating because you can set the highest standards possible for the completion of your work in order to satisfy the enterprise's objectives. The success of the completion of your work will always be a guarantee that you will be paid.

There are some jobs that do not pay the same amount of money working out of an office rather than being a freelancer. Working remotely allows you to capitalize on the benefits of delivering good work each time as compared to most office jobs that recognize employee achievements after extended durations of time.

It is possible to achieve maximum happiness with your job as a result of always delivering on time. You will be able to get your money based on each task completed, and this minimizes the amount of time spent waiting for your paycheck at the end of the week or month.

You will be in a position to keep track of your actual productivity each time you set to work. The disadvantage of not working remotely is that you will constantly have a supervisor who will regulate the amount of work you can do. Consequently, you might not get recognized for each completed yield of work, but there is a large sense of satisfaction when you work remotely to success.

As long as you are working hard, strictly maintaining a schedule and getting the desired results, you will be able to get paid much faster than somebody working in an office waiting for their salary. There is a greater sense of satisfaction with doing things by yourself that creates a profitable working culture.

If you know that you can constantly produce results and ensure the success of an enterprise, consider working remotely as you will be paid upon the completion of every job. While in an office you will have to work towards a definite schedule, working remotely allows you to set your own time.

Another important advantage of working remotely that guides you towards the path of entrepreneurship is working and managing teams effectively. In today's world, technological advancements have allowed us to have access to different effective ways of communicating.

Most people have to work out of an office because they have to work as a team and constantly communicate. However, if there is nothing attaching these employees physically, they might as well work remotely and employ one of the more effective ways of communicating with each other.

Video chats and conferences have become particularly popular among business people and employees who have to work in different locations. Take an example of large multinational corporations that have employees spread out across the world.

When there is a need for such employees to communicate or even the management arm of the business, video conferences have become the most effective way of relying on information. There is no need for anybody to hop onto a jet simply to go and conduct business in another country.

It is now possible to communicate over large distances and still communicate information effectively. This means that working remotely should be the preference as it brings together employees from all over the world. There is now no reason or employees to meet if there is urgent information that has to be communicated.

Therefore, working as a team has become even more effective. While it is good enough enjoying the physical presence of your workmates, it limits the amount of time you can work together because you can only handle office matters during office hours.

However, working remotely allows you to keep in touch with your fellow employees and business accomplices at any time if need be. If the information has come through at the dead hours of the night, it is still possible to relay information and work on a challenge even before meeting up with fellow workmates the following morning.

Most people have come to appreciate the freedom they can enjoy by working from home because they can still manage teams effectively. The communication means available to remote workers mean that they can conduct team work sessions with even greater precision because every member of the team will be within their comfort zone.

Productivity certainly increases as a result of workers having a comfortable working environment in which to maximize their yields. Allowing the manifestation of remote work in professional life streamlines team work and also makes it possible to manage the efforts of each person.

There is no need to maintain the physical presence of your workers if you are an employer because you can still keep track of their activities online. This is particularly useful if you develop an intranet for your enterprise that allows you to constantly maintain access to your employees.

Similarly, if employees have a single job portal from which they can access their work, it is also possible to manage their work efforts by controlling the access to information they have about the enterprise. This allows them to remain productive in their specific field of work to guarantee success.

When you work remotely, you create a lot of time for yourself that offers the opportunity to learn new skills. You do not have to restrict yourself to what you majored in college; if there is an opportunity o learn a new skill, at least you will be working remotely where nobody will restrict your actions.

Remote work exposes most people to new professions and even new business opportunities. This often requires learning a new skill in order to specialize in a particular trade. It is almost impossible for an office worker to spend time learning a new skill while they are working with their colleagues.

For instance, if you feel that you can provide services better for your clients by learning how to speak French, it will be possible to set some time each day to learn the language. Working remotely means that nobody will question your actions as long as you are able to maintain your work yields.

However, if you are working in an office, you will find that there is no time to learn a new language even if it might improve your work. You will be under constant supervision and it will affect your approach to succeeding in your work.

You will be constantly interrupted if you are in an office trying to learn a new skill, and as long as it is not part of the overall objectives of the business, you are likely to be told you are in violation of the terms of your own contract.

Remote work exposes the individual to a chance of self improvement because they can manage their time in such a manner as to allow this. You will have no supervisors breathing down on your neck, and you will be able to spend time pursuing things that actually interest you.

When you start doing work remotely, you will infinitely realize that there are several aspects of your operation that you will need to improve. If you are working for an organization from home, you will find that they have suitable training programs that you can access from home and improve yourself.

Several large corporations that have remote workers post training modules online so that employees can spend time with them to completely understand what they need. Spending time alone in training forces you to do your own research to improve your own work yields.

The training programs accessible by most companies can help you boost your own business as you head down the path of entrepreneurship. There is something unique about learning by yourself without the pressure of a supervisor as it makes the experience much more exciting.

You will find that most remote workers have much more refined skills for tackling their work than the office worker who has probably attended all train sessions in the organization. A remote worker will always improve themselves beyond normal convention and they will focus on aspects of their job that they actually enjoy.

Overall, you can never doubt your income when you are working remotely because despite having fun, you will still be getting your paychecks. There will barely be any difference between you and the office worker who also has to wait until the end of the week for their salary.

If you are harboring plans of starting your own business but you are still at work, consider joining that business first as a remote worker. This will give you a chance to maintain your income while at the same time learning everything about the business you are interested in.

If you are a tax collector but you want to start a job selling books online, consider being an e-book writer and specialize in writing topics that you are actually good at. Look for a self publishing author you can write with or look through several job search engines for an appropriate writing job.

You will be amazed by the amount of information you can collect while working at a simple job online. You will be able to learn of its disadvantages and advantages even before venturing into it, and by the time you have spent a couple of months doing it, you will be far educated about it than before.

Remote work is not only an opportunity to make more money doing what you love, but it is also a chance for you to increase your knowledge. A successful entrepreneur identifies business risks that are likely to change their approach to doing business and mitigate them immediately.

When you opt to work remotely, particularly if you are quitting your normal desk job, you expose yourself to a whole new world of possibilities that you did not think existed. You will be able to decide on appropriate businesses to start because you are already in them and understand how they operate.

As an entrepreneur, there is no better place to start than working remotely. By the time you are establishing your business, you already have adequate experience to get past most challenges you will encounter and you can make solid business decisions based on the knowledge you have already collected.

It is also useful to do a remote job because it will open up your thinking and allow you to come up with new products. Experience is a crucial part of any successful entrepreneurship and once you are in a position to present viable new products to the market, you will never return to employment again.

When you start working remotely, you eliminate other common problems that the typical desk office worker goes through every day. One of the most notable problems you will be getting rid of by sitting in the house and being productive is avoiding the normal hassles of a daily commute.

If you drive yourself to work, consider the amount of gas you use on a daily basis. As an entrepreneur, you will quickly realize that this is a large and unnecessary expense that constantly subtracts from you without a significant benefit.

If you can work from home, why burn all that fuel on a daily basis. That is money that can be used expanding your business; restrict your car travels to emergencies and actual physical meetings that you cannot avoid because driving to work every day is too much of a hassle.

Remote workers can wake up in the wee hours of the morning, get to do their work in the stillness of the moment and go back to sleep when commuters are waking up to go to work. There is no pleasurable feeling than being comfortably in your house on a cold Monday morning sleeping without a care in the world.

Indeed, a famous Indian saying states that a successful person is one who can spend an entire day by the banks of a river without feeling guilty about it. If you have to be at work but you are spending too much time enjoying yourself in a restaurant, you are likely to feel very guilty about it.

You have bills to pay, food to buy and a lifestyle to uphold. If you are not working, you will become nervous because it means you will not be able to meet basic expenses in your life. This will prompt you to immediately stop enjoying yourself so that you can go to work.

However, that individual who wakes up in the morning and spends the entire time in front of a television screen eating cereals but has a successful business is the happiest of all people. The end game of entrepreneurship is for your money to work for you, and this can be achieved first by starting to work remotely.

If you can eliminate the time you spend on your daily commutes, you will find that a significant amount of time has suddenly opened up in your life. Consider doing a remote job because, at least, nobody tells you when you have to leave your own house.

You will be surprised that you can increase your work yields while working from home rather than reporting to an office on a daily basis. This is because you are in a better position to focus on what really has to be completed with minimal distractions.

In an office, you have to deal with the normal employee politics and you also have to demarcate time to speak with your colleagues. Lunch breaks in an office are deemed essential, but the simple fact is, they are time consuming and can be spent in a much more productive way.

If you are working from out of your home, you do not have to spend an entire hour eating lunch. You can prepare yourself in advance such that you constantly have food to eat, and you do not have to have specific hours for eating. You can enjoy a meal at any time as long as you are working hard.

This means that there is an excellent chance for your work productivity to increase immensely. You do not have anybody but yourself pressuring you, and this creates a much more comfortable environment for completing your tasks to precision.

In a similar fashion, it becomes possible for you to boost your concentration when working because of the reduced distractions. If your work requires you to think intensely or be creative, then working a remote job should be the best option for you.

As an employer, you will find that it is much easier to retain your employees if they are working from home than if they have to constantly report to work. Your employees will enjoy their work even if they do not enjoy the specific assignments they have to do because they have the freedom to control themselves.

Most employees end up losing their jobs because they are unable to relate well with their fellow employees or their boss. But if they are working from home, the human resources aspect of the work is entirely up to them, and their productivity will be based on their own hard working nature and not pressure from you as the employer.

When you are working remotely, some basic problems such as the very nature of your office stop becoming a problem. This is because your office can be on any kind, from working in your living room, renting out a hotel or even working from your bedroom.

You cannot be restricted from where to work when you are working remotely. Take the example of the inspiring story of J. K. Rowling, one of the wealthiest authors in the world. When she started writing the series that has famously become known as 'Harry Potter,' she claimed to be doing some of her writing out of coffee shops.

She would get into her local coffee shop, ask for a cup and proceed to work seated there. Despite all the distractions around her, she was able to 'convert' some of the coffee shops she visited into her offices, and the result was a massive success and her name being known all over the world.

In fact, J. K. Rowling claimed that the idea of the book came to her while she was on a train trip in the United Kingdom. The idea came to her literally as she was travelling, and she had to look for a notepad to scribble down her ideas and set the foundation for what would become one of the most successfully sold books in the world.

The success that J. K. Rowling managed should be an example for any entrepreneur regardless of the industry they are operating in. This is because you can convert almost anywhere into an office, and the advantage is that you will be in full control of your own work yield.

Another advantage of working remotely is that you do not have to restrict yourself in a single location. It is possible for you to work from almost anywhere across the world as long as you can access the basic resources you need to complete your work.

Remote work just might be the solution for rural to urban migration that has resulted in the neglect of the countryside. In the twentieth century, large masses of the populations have been moving to urban areas mainly in search of jobs and better working opportunities.

Rural areas have come to be associated as centers for agriculture and other activities that normally do not happen in the big cities. They are extremely spacious, particularly now in the twenty-first century as the growth of cities has been accelerating through the decades.

You can opt to move to a rural area to conduct your work, and chances are that you will e joy the experience immensely. As compared to working in the city, rural areas are far much quieter and the quality of the air is also quite different.

You can manage to achieve a great sense of comfort by opting to work away from the city particularly if you have no obligations there. A rural area will have all the space you need, and some basic things such as food and rent are also likely to be much cheaper.

You also do not have to be restricted in your country of origin; the beginning of a remote job is the beginning of a life of travel, and this means you can live anywhere on the globe as long as you are in a position to work. Remote jobs are all about results, not the location from which you are working.

It is much easier to keep in touch with fellow workers and even prospective business partners when you are working remotely. Think of all the people you have encountered at some point in your life who are difficult to get even on the phone simply because of the demanding nature of their daytime jobs.

With a remote worker, it will be easier to communicate with them because they are not reporting to anybody in particular. You can ask them for assistance at almost any time because they are responsible for managing their own time, unlike office workers whose time management is in the hands of supervisors.

There are so many platforms of communication that ensure the remote worker is more informed than the office worker. As a remote worker, you have the freedom to go over several sources of information to know what is happening around you without too many problems.

Overall, you will find that your general sense of happiness will increase tremendously as a result of working remotely. You do not have to ensure the normal stress of working in an office because there are several people to relate with and there are strict rules to abide by.

A remote worker is likely to have a big smile on their faces at the end of the day because they will have controlled their own time and be able to achieve comfort while working. It is possible for them to display a bigger sense of happiness than their colleagues working in an office.

The general stress levels associated with working in an office are completely avoided by working remotely. One of the fundamental aspects that help improve work yields among employees is happiness; as long as workers are happy and in an appreciative mood, then it is likely that they will complete their work more effectively than the office worker whose time has to be regulated.

In summary working remotely will teach you time management, how to work in teams, how to work and get paid based on results. All these skills are vital when starting your own business. You will also have a flexible schedule with a steady paycheck which you can use to invest in your business.

Chapter 2: What Type of Remote Jobs Are Available

There are a limitless number of jobs available that you can access to work remotely, preferably from home.

In the past couple of years, more than fifty percent of employment across the world can be attributed to remote work. This statistic is a stark contrast to only ten percent in the nineties when remote work started gaining ground, and it was less than five percent of the total job market in the eighties.

Remote work has been gaining popularity mainly because of the advancements of the internet as well as technological changes. The internet has made the entire world one small community because it is possible to communicate in real time with anybody from around the world.

There has been an increasing trend of people conducting their purchases online, further cementing the need for remote jobs to take off. Most people are now able to do jobs they once had to go to the office to complete from the comfort of their homes with similar, if not more success.

Most businesses attributed eighty percent of their sales to the internet. Having an online presence has become so important that there are several remote jobs that have emerged to help keep up with the demand. These jobs are slowly replacing traditional office desk jobs.

In today's world, an increasing number of businesses are turning to remote workers because they display more advantages than having a constant office staff. Remote jobs are projected to increase to seventy percent of the job market by 2020.

One of the advantages that big businesses see with hiring remote workers is that it enables them to save up on extra expenses. Maintaining an office staff is far more expensive than having remote workers who work from the comfort of their homes.

Having an office staff means paying rent for the premises, supplying additional resources to facilitate their work and even purchasing different stationery to streamline the work. When the business hires workers remotely, they eliminate so many major expenses that otherwise reduce their profits.

Another crucial reason why so many businesses are turning to remote workers is that they are able to access the best talent not only within their premises but from around the world. The internet is the perfect place for hiring very skilled individuals who will contribute significantly to your business without you ever meeting them.

Remote workers from around the world are easily accessible to big businesses, and they can seek to find the best workers to support their enterprise. It is possible to find the best skills in the world by relying on remote workers, and it is also likely to be cheaper because labor costs vary across the world.

Several big businesses now maintain a large staff that is competent to the specific operations of the enterprise. The management has an opportunity to look through the largest pool of workers they possibly can in order to select the most suitable people to support their profitability ventures.

Remote workers also have helped several businesses achieve a 24-hour working regime because remote workers can work through the entire day. Outsourcing different laborers from across the world enable businesses to take advantage of time differences and ensure their workers constantly remain productive.

This is an extremely good strategy for big businesses because it ensures that they maximize every single hour on productivity. This will not be possible if they have office staff and even if they hire enough employees, the overhead costs will be tremendous as compare to having remote workers.

It is estimated that by 2025, a majority of corporations across the world will consist of 70 percent of their work force being remote workers. From accountants, developers, and marketers, most of their employees will have the chance of working from the comfort of their homes.

The working environment is going to change significantly in the next few years because it will almost be impossible to find people working in an office. Only those jobs that require people to physically meet will retain offices, otherwise, most of the traditional jobs that people had to go to work in a building will soon disappear.

Most people prefer to work from home, anyway because it makes them more productive. They can utilize their time in an effective manner to ensure that they maximize their output and produce far larger yields than they would if they were constantly going to an office.

Similarly, concentration levels increase because there are fewer distractions when somebody decides to work remotely. Remote workers have the privilege of choosing where they want to work from and this makes it very simple for them to work hard to reasonable success.

One of the more common remote jobs available that almost anybody can do is that of an email marketer. The responsibility of such a professional is to spread advertisements for different products and services by contacting clients via email.

It can be a strenuous job because you have to keep up with a multitude of people, but it is quite rewarding because affiliate companies have different compensation schemes available for their employees. You can do this job comfortably from home by simply acquiring a laptop and a stable internet connection.

There is nothing complicated about email marketing because some businesses provide you with a template or advertisements to present to clients. Such institutions might take advantage of the number of followers you have but they are likely to reimburse you based on this fact, as well.

Email marketing is something that has gained prominence over the past few years and it is popular because it directly targets single clients. It is an effective way of spreading the word about new or unique products in the market because it is a personalized message to each prospective client.

Another job that is gaining popularity in the remote work industry is that of promotional video makers. This is a job title that is becoming so popular due to the number of streaming channels and promotional video websites that have come up throughout the world.

For instance, millions of videos are uploaded onto YouTube every single day, meaning that promotional video makers have a big opportunity to land lucrative job opportunities. This is one job that almost anybody can do as long as they are familiar with basic promotional strategies.

Freelance writing is another lucrative job opportunity that is available for those who want to work remotely. There are several approaches to freelance writing that an individual can exploit depending on their preferences and level of skill.

One of the most lucrative forms of freelance remote writing jobs is ghostwriting. This is a job where a writer is provided with instructions on the type of book or article to write but hand over the rights of the book to the purchaser. The writer is never acknowledged for their work apart from the paycheck they will receive.

Ghostwriters earn anywhere from three thousand dollars a month to hundreds, if not millions, of dollars. There are several publishing companies that are looking for competent writers who can provide quality manuscripts depending on their needs and they always compensate ghostwriters well.

There are autobiographical and biographical writers who are also in high demand. Depending on the type of publisher you find, it is possible to also make a lucrative salary working remotely. Such writers usually have to work closely with the people they are writing about, and they always get good compensation for the amount of time they spend on a project.

Freelance remote writing jobs can also include article writers who prepare advertisements, informative articles and website content for the benefit of different clients. It is simple enough to find these jobs but writers usually have to go through an initial screening process before accessing work.

Blog writers also have important jobs to do online and they provide information to a string of followers. This is also a lucrative remote job, provided you set up your enterprise well so that many people can find you online. Blog writing can be done at anytime and does not require a strict schedule.

Remote writing jobs provide a bulk of the work that people can do easily online and get paid. Most of these jobs pay on a daily and weekly basis, making them effective income earners to your current job. Most people turn to freelance writing because the market currently is insatiable for new content.

Another lucrative job opportunity that can be one easily from home is that of a web and graphic designer. These individuals have some of the best remote jobs because they get to practice what they really like for pay. This is another job that is also in constant demand because new content emerges on the internet every hour.

Graphic designers can work for a large company or for a single individual. They can do all their work from the house an there is a creasing number of graphic designers who actually have to report to an office. It is a specialized skill and requires several hours of practice, but it is a lucrative income earner for anybody who specializes in it.

Web designers are also in constant demand and if you were to leave your job today, you will not be short of a lucrative market. Websites are coming up on the internet as frequently as videos and other forms of entertainment are uploaded online.

There is a lot of work for web designers, particularly when there are upgrades to various forms of technology that allows for unique websites to come up. The internet is awash with billions of websites and all of them require web designers to customize for use for different people and enterprises.

Translators are also opening up their services to online sources, making it easy to work from home. Translators do not have to report to an office particularly when they can utilize video messages as well as the internet to help their clients understand different languages.

There are two types of translators; there are writers who are tasked with the responsibility of converting texts into a different language. This job is easy enough and only requires a laptop with internet connectivity, and the translator can work from anywhere at their convenience.

There are verbal translators who have to ensure their clients understand different conversations in different situations. A translator in this instance can maintain contact with their client and provide live translation as their client listens to another person speaking in a language they do not understand.

Translators are paid very well depending on the individuals and companies they work for. It is a simple job particularly for anybody who has knowledge of more than two languages. They can put this simple understanding to practice for a very lucrative reward.

Customer service management is another job opportunity that is growing tremendously for freelancers in the past few years. According to statistics from Yale University, the percentage of customer care representatives online has increased twice fold in the last five years alone.

There are many opportunities for customer care representatives as businesses increase their online presence and rely on social media platforms to communicate with their clients. The customer care representatives can do their work from anywhere in the world and represent any type of organization.

Technological advancements have made it efficient for customers to communicate directly with a business and even shop online. This means that the need for customer representatives to be at the physical location of a business is negligible.

This is a lucrative earner for anybody looking to work remotely, and the qualifications for these jobs are also minimal. Anybody who can speak fluently and confidently with customers is eligible to work in such a job, and if they find several clients, they can make thousands of dollars every month.

The roles for transcribers online are also increasing because most people are looking for remote workers to complete these jobs. Converting speech to text is a lucrative job opportunity at does not require strict qualifications and almost anybody can do it.

It is possible to find several transcribing opportunities that will earn significant amounts of money every week, and it is a perfect way of working remotely. The needs for such a job are also quite reduced as all you will need is a laptop computer and a stable internet connection.

Crowd sourcing is also another important opportunity for people looking to work remotely because it involves raising money online for different types of projects. Crowd sourcing managers can raise money for upcoming book projects, a business idea that needs to be implemented or even raise money for charity.

These opportunities do not require specialized knowledge to complete because all a prospective crowd sourcing manager will require is a laptop and steady internet connectivity. Most crowd sourcing opportunities today are being funded by large corporations, making it a lucrative earner for anybody looking to quit their day time job and start working for themselves.

According to Fortune 500, Android and iPhone developers have been on the increase in the past few years, making up a significant percentage of remote freelance workers online. If you are tech savvy and understand the basic requirements for developing Android apps and iPhones, then you have a lucrative job opportunity working remotely.

Most developers get hired by large companies to improve their products, and each assignment can be worth thousands of dollars. You will need a solid background in software engineering and computer science to be successful in this work, but it will surely pay you very well.

If you are looking to quit your desk job and start working from home profitably, then consider being an accountant. Although this is a specialist profession that requires at least a business degree and a good understanding of math, it is an extremely lucrative remote job.

A majority of the large companies across the world are relying on remote accountants more and more because of the cheap overhead expenses and their practicability. Most accountants today choose to work from home, maintaining offices only when they need to physically meet some of their clients.

Remote accountants still earn hundreds of thousands of dollars each year despite working from home. The general assumption is that they will be more comfortable working from a quiet place where they have fewer distractions and a better chance of reducing errors in their reports.

Another profession that is equally popular but requires some specialist knowledge is that of nurses. Surprisingly, there are a huge number of remote nurses working from their own homes across the United States tending to different patients.

It is surprising for such a job to be remote considering it sometimes requires a hands-on approach. However, specialist nurses are able to care for their patients right from home because they rely on sophisticated technology that allows them to keep track of their patients, requiring them to physically meet them only when the need arises.

Otherwise, there is a huge percentage of nurses working across the United States helping patients suffering from different ailments, and this is in line with the general need to boost standards of health care in the country. Thus, if you have the qualifications, consider doing this job remotely.

Nurses who work remotely are still compensated handsomely and it is an excellent way of earning a living. With the direction that technology is heading, there will be fewer nurses working directly from the hospital and a huge number working throughout the country remotely.

Skilled engineers can also easily work out of their houses because their presence on most sites is not a requirement. Engineers can draw up blueprints, write up a list of requirements and provide important information to ensure the continuation of a project.

This has been witnessed with some Chinese contractors who have provided information for the construction of road networks across Africa via video conferences. Some engineers do not even have to be in the field, opting to divulge crucial information through an established communication system.

This is an excellent remote position for a skilled engineer because they still get reimbursed in a similar manner as on-site engineers. For skilled engineers, they have a chance of making even more money because they can advertise their services online and acquire clients from all over the world.

The teaching profession is another lucrative remote job that has millions of employees spread across the internet. Teachers, tutors, and instructors all perform a similar role and they help different types of students with their studies to attain degrees from various learning institutions.

The tutors that can be found online have several students who they provide assistance and guidance to pass certain courses. Most institutions now have an option for long distance students to learn and attain a degree online.

This has diversified the teaching profession in a big way and opened up doors of opportunity for individuals who have an interest in this profession. With the latest technological advancements, going to class will soon become irrelevant because teachers can conduct their jobs remotely.

If you have an interest in being a tutor, it is important to know that you stand to make lots of money. You do not have to be restricted to a single learning institution, you can help tutor students from all over the world. This has brought massive changes to the profession and made it a lucrative income earner.

Consultancy is another profession that has gained popularity through the years as an increasing number of advisers operate remotely. Several clients prefer to have a consultant who operates remotely because it is easier to keep in touch with them as compared to constantly going to visit them in their office.

Consultancy is also a lucrative profession because there are different types of consultancies that you can open. Depending on the prevailing demand in a market, consultants can ensure they have constant business by working remotely to give them access to clients from all over the world.

Several companies require consultants for all sorts of professions; legal consultants, business consultants, and even health consultants. With the right qualifications, a consultancy will lead you to the path of entrepreneurship because you will open up your own business and quit your full time job.

Program and project managers are also increasingly working out of their homes because their presence is sometimes not necessary in most projects. Program managers are responsible for providing the technical aspects of a project and delegating important responsibilities to appropriate persons.

All this can be done remotely and it is upon them to analyze the statistics of the project to determine if it is achieving success. The jobs of program managers are highly coveted because they pay well and they give the employee a chance to work from anywhere in the world.

If you are savvy at business and probably have long experience working for a top organization, you should consider marketing your skills and working remotely. With the advent of the internet, there are an increasing number of businesses popping online as more customers prefer to do their shopping remotely.

As a business development manager, you will be responsible for offering financial advice, preparing business reports and giving your clients forecasts for their enterprises. This is a very lucrative position if you are experienced because you can be approached by a large company to offer financial advice.

Most emerging businesses prefer to work with experienced professionals who can provide appropriate information to assist their companies to prosper, and this is an excellent position to consider working from home.

There are several headhunting companies that can be found online, and they are responsible for recruitment strategies for several businesses around the world. Most companies see the human resource sector of their business as being expendable as far as recruitment is concerned.

With a large number of viable recruiters easily being found remotely, it is possible to access an even larger pool of skilled employees who would be a good fit for any organization. If you have the connection and resources, consider opening a website where you assist different people to get their dream jobs.

Sales representatives also work remotely in the changing

business world. Since it is possible to conduct successful sales promotions online, most sales representatives avail their services on the internet and help different types of businesses and individuals market their products and services.

Sales representatives are sometimes paid on commission, but it is also possible to negotiate a one-off fee with your client. This is a profession that has been increasing in numbers remotely because of the ease of conducting different promotional strategies while being in a remote location.

Most sales representatives rely on the internet to conduct their work because they can advertise different products and services via social media platforms. Some sales representatives already have several clients they have served in the past and will use them to advertise new products and services.

If done continuously, sales representatives make several hundreds of thousands of dollars every year. It is a full time job and one that requires a lot of time but it is an excellent replacement for your day time job because you will be remunerated excellently.

There is also an increasing number of data analysts who are working remotely and earning goo money every year. Data analysts do not have to be in an office to perform their responsibilities and the requirements of the job are usually not that complicated.

As long as you are tech savvy and have access to a laptop and stable internet connection, you can learn all about data analysis and be able to prepare reports for different clients from the comfort of your home. In fact, most businesses now prefer to have their data analysts work remotely because the advantages far outweigh the disadvantages.

Several editors are now working remotely and this is another profession that shows a lot of promise. Editing jobs are numerous all over the internet because there is a constant need to fix different kinds of manuscripts. Editing jobs still require people to spend a lot of time, but hey remunerate well when you find the right employer.

There are no shortages of these jobs and all you need to do if find out the topics that best suit you and search for the jobs. There are numerous different types of clients, from single individuals to large companies that are constantly seeking good editors for their content.

If you are good at doing research, consider research engineering because this is another job whose online presence is increasing progressively. Research engineering involves looking into a specific topic or subject of discussion and preparing a report.

All you will need to complete most of these assignments is a stable internet connection and a laptop computer. It is also important that you are familiar with the various research methods and formats as this will be instrumental in the presentation of your final report to your client.

Advertisement is a growing business on the internet, and if you are familiar with SEO writing, then you have a chance of joining a lucrative profession. SEO specialists essentially prepare key words for different websites that will help guide anybody searching for a specific product or service.

The key words increase the total traffic a website can experience, and this is crucial for the success of any online business. Thus, SEO specialists are well paid and they can work from anywhere in the world. Their job is simple enough as all that is required is a good internet connection and a laptop computer.

There are several job websites where individuals can access these remote jobs. Some of these websites include We Work Remotely and Upwork. They host different types of clients requiring specific remote services, and this gives a chance for freelancers to bid on projects they feel competent to complete.

Remote jobs require a surprising amount of dedication because the individual must discipline themselves to be productive. It is important that they understand the various challenges associated with working remotely because time must be spent in the best way possible to guarantee success.

The simple fact remains that even the job you are currently doing will eventually become remote sooner or later. With the current technological advancements, there is a limitless number of jobs that you can access and quit your full time job. It is possible to achieve immense success working remotely as you would working in an office job.

Most people have a permanent employment status in several organizations yet they ever once report o the premises. Some employees are located overseas but remain crucial to the success that the company can achieve. You should aspire to be one of these individuals because you will be able to live life much more comfortably working from home.

The stigma surrounding remote jobs is slowly disappearing as more and more people are realizing the benefits of working from home. When the stay-at-home dad emerged onto the social scene for the first time, it was a cause for harsh whispers and even criticism for laziness.

In the present world, stay-at home dads are perhaps the most successful of employees because they get to work in the comfort of their homes and determine their own schedules. They are much happier than when they used to go to an office and they are capable of reaching new heights.

It is necessary not to restrict yourself to a single profession because new remote jobs are emerging even today. It does not have to be a professional role that has long been an office ob and finally becoming remote; new types of responsibilities are emerging and remote jobs offer the solution for most companies.

E-book publishers, for example, are increasing because almost anybody can open a publishing website online. There is an increasing market for these books worldwide and it has led to people being creative and creating this profession.

Publishing has long been something that has been controlled by the traditional forms of media. It has been very difficult for new writers to get recognized if a traditional publisher does not select their works for publishing and selling.

This form of publishing, therefore, is a remote job in itself and it will be a lucrative earner once you find a host of readers who want to purchase different types of books. Publishing online has opened up all sorts of professions such as marketing, and if this is your fit, you will never be out of work.

The vastness of remote jobs across the world has transformed it into an excellent alternative to the traditional jobs that are becoming scarcer by the day. By working remotely, you will be supporting the principles of several businesses and thus you will rarely lack work to do.

When you start working remotely, you are taking the initial steps towards becoming an entrepreneur because successful remote work often results in the opening a business. Regardless of the profession, you are engaged in when you successfully work remotely, expansion is inevitable.

It is necessary to find out more about entrepreneurship because you will soon move from being an employee to being an employer. The key aspect of success as far as remote work is concerned is to do a profession that you are most familiar with and makes you happy. There is no point engaging in a profession that does not interest you because it will attract failure.

Choose wisely when you start a remote job because it has the propensity to completely change your life.

Chapter 3: How to Get Your First Remote Jobs

When you make the decision to get a remote job, you might be puzzled at the process involved.

However, getting a remote job is not difficult at all; in fact, all you need is to have an excellent presentation and to know where to look. There are numerous types of remote jobs available out there, it is highly unlikely that you will not find one that suits you.

When looking for a remote job, remember it is important to know exactly what you want to do so that you can make your search more precise. It is necessary to know exactly where you will be looking and the sort of job that is suitable in occupying your time.

The first step in finding a remote job is sitting down by yourself and thinking hard about how you want to spend your time over the next year. Some people are too hasty finding a remote job that they settle for anything and quickly realize that their time and expertise is needed more than they thought.

The simple truth is, remote jobs are complex and require your maximum attention if you want some serious money. When you start working remotely, it is not an excuse for sitting down at home and spending the entire day relaxing and watching television.

Actually, you might find yourself being more occupied with your job than before. This is because you will have more responsibilities with a remote job because your boss will expect you to supervise yourself and guarantee high quality when you are finally submitting in your work.

The first step you should take when looking for remote jobs is looking through the job boards.

There are a tremendous number of them on the internet depending on the industry you want to work for, and you will no doubt find an abundance of jobs fitted to you.

The job boards will give you an insight into the basic requirements of most employers and the nature of the jobs. Your first step should be to look through as many of them as possible, marking out the most suitable for you to use in search of jobs that seem appropriate to you.

There are different types of job boards that you will immediately encounter such as Glassdoor, Craigslist and Indeed. However, you will need to look for those that will allow you to maximize the most appropriate remote jobs so as to free you up from your current employment position.

One of the more popular job boards for remote workers is We Work Remotely. It is a simple website that is easy to maneuver, and some of the main jobs that you will be able to find on it include web design, customer service, and programming jobs.

The site hosts up to 130,000 different telecommuters, and it is quite convenient for those looking for simple remote jobs that pay regularly. The site is popular and has received some stellar recommendations, and so it might be useful to consider it when looking for remote jobs.

For female job seekers who want to work from home and quit their day time jobs, PowerToFly is an excellent website to check out. The website mainly specializes in tech jobs and it looks to provide pertinent information to female job seekers to match them with appropriate remote jobs.

There are many other types of jobs that female job seekers can also look for on this website. It has comprehensive information on the best approaches for finding remote jobs, making it a very useful tool for those looking to replace their desk jobs.

FlexJobs is a large website that is equally useful for remote workers from a diverse range. The website offers visitors a choice from 50 different categories of remote jobs, making t appropriate for anybody looking to start out for the first time to browse on the different opportunities available.

Remote.co is also another useful website worth checking out because it also lists numerous remote jobs suitable for those looking for constant income. This website specializes in job categories such as developer jobs, customer service positions, sales jobs, recruiter and HR roles, design opportunities, and other remote work, including managers, marketers, and writers.

Justremote.co is also another website that is worth checking out because it has useful information for those who are starting out in remote jobs. The website is known for connecting designers, web developers as well as marketers to different legitimate job opportunities, making it appropriate for those who are just starting out.

The above websites are just but a few of the options available for remote job seekers to explore. It is important to settle for job boards that display the kind of jobs you are interested in rather than forcing yourself to work in an industry that you are not well versed in.

It is of absolute importance to remain patient in the search for a job. The simple fact is that there are numerous jobs being posted on these boards and keeping track of them can be challenging. Settling for an industry that you are not familiar with might eventually discourage you from looking for remote jobs.

It is important that the job you do makes you feel comfortable and is one with minimal hassles for you. The whole point of leaving your desk job is to make life more comfortable for yourself. It will be possible to achieve this by using the job boards to the greatest effect to ensure you find a job that suits your abilities.

Remember that you will need to do some practice on your presentation. You must especially work on your own pitch, understanding what is appropriate to include in an email or when speaking to a potential recruiter.

It is important to provide as much information about yourself as possible, but try to keep it relevant to the actual job you are applying for. Job recruiters like to see that the prospective candidates are following clear instructions they have provided and are respectful in their responses.

You also have to prepare your remote presentation in terms of your online presence. A prospective client who is interested in your service will want to learn more about you, and so posting your information in an appropriate manner will enable them to learn what they need.

Make sure your social media accounts are presentable to the extent that an employer can go through your profile comfortably. You should also provide appropriate information about yourself so that a prospective employer has a rough image of the type of person you are.

Be sure to include past projects in your portfolio that will help convince a prospective employer to hire you. Most employers like to see somebody who already has some kind of experience handling the same type of work they are doing. This is instrumental in landing you a deal particularly when you are starting out.

It does not matter whether some of the work you have done was professional or not, what is important is that you have some experience handling it. An employer will consequently feel comfortable hiring you because your portfolio displays key experiences that will help you achieve success with remote work.

As much as you are working remotely, there is one aspect of getting hired that will not change in comparison to normal desk jobs. When you want to contact an employer, it is necessary to be strictly professional from your first response and other communication thereafter.

You have to prepare a cover letter and a resume that highlights your experiences and your interest in the job opportunity. However, be sure to follow instructions to the latter because there are a few employers who will not request a resume immediately.

A great resume has a number of requirements that if you follow, you will be able to prepare an excellent document. The first thing you have to know is that you have to be strictly professional and formal in the resume; do not write as though you are trying to have a conversation with the recipient.

Instead, present yourself in such a manner as to show you are ready to work. You have to use the normal standard format of most resumes, observing simple guidelines such as using A4 paper and making sure the font is strictly black.

Use simple language, avoid complicated jargon. Most job seekers usually want to show that they are well versed for a specific job by using difficult terminology in their resumes. If you find yourself preparing a resume with the help of a dictionary, you are probably overdoing it.

When preparing the resume, adopt a simplistic tone that highlights your qualifications for the job and paste experiences that are relevant to the position. Using difficult language will not help you because a prospective employer will determine your suitability for the position based on your qualifications.

It is very important to ensure that your contact information is absolutely clear and legible. This is something that people sometimes ignore, and it can be devastating if an employer is interested in your services but cannot contact you because you have not left the relevant information in the cover letter and resume.

Your contact information should go on the upper right hand corner of the A4 paper, starting out with your name, your address, your telephone number and email address is need be. Below that but on the left hand corner of the same page, include the name and address of the recipient of the cover letter.

Make sure that the overall presentation of the resume is meticulous; use a font that is large enough to be read without a struggle but not too large enough that only a few lines occupy one page. A neat presentation is an extremely important factor to ensure is implemented in your document.

You have to be able to clearly state your experience because this is the one thing that prospective employers will focus on. If the experience of the prospective candidate is not clear from their resume, then the prospective employer will assume the candidate will be unable to handle tasks handed down to them.

You have to emphasize how you will contribute to the job that you are applying for when preparing the resume. This is important because the prospective employer wants to see that you have followed their instructions and understand the nature of work that is involved.

When you prepare a resume, try to make a custom made one for each job that you apply. Most people make the mistake of preparing a standard resume that sometimes might include irrelevant information to some employers. Make sure to make a custom made resume for every job position you apply for.

With this in mind, read through the basic instructions for each of the jobs you apply for before sending in a resume. Each job will have specific requirements based on your initial response, and if you are unable to spot these requirements, it will rule you from landing the remote job.

Displaying your competence for a remote job will be determined right from the cover letter you present and the general layout of your resume. Employers like to see job seekers who take their position seriously and are able to follow basic instructions for the job. You will endear yourself to a prospective employer by following instructions alone.

You should also state your current job situation to an employer as they always value this information to know whether you have any experience. Stating your current job situation might also allow your prospective employer to give you a flexible remote schedule so that you can be working only at specific hours.

Your current job situation will also let your employer know other important things such as the type of work you are familiar with handling. This will make it easy for them to place you within their organization to a job suited for you once you land a job with them.

Make sure not to drag out information in your resume; keep things short and brief, but also keep in mind that sharing relevant information about yourself is just as important. Make sure you include relevant aspects about yourself without missing out on the important bits.

Make sure your employer is familiar with your education history because he is one thing people sometimes skip in their resumes. Some people have lengthy resumes highlighting the different jobs they have done, but they do not include their education history.

For a business operating remotely, the owners will like to know that the employees they are hiring are at least qualified and knowledgeable to handle the jobs they will be given. Since there will be little chance of meeting, it is necessary that you ensure your employer knows your education history comprehensively.

Finally, and most important of all, a great resume should be sent in an appropriate manner following the instructions for sending. There are some employers who might require physical copies of some of your documents as well as the resume and cover letters, and so you will have to send these by post.

If an employer has provided an email address, use it; do not phone them in to ask them if there is an alternative way for you to send in your resume. Most employers usually present this information clearly in the job advert and so you should not question it.

Your resume should also follow a general structure that allows it to be appropriate. After presenting your address and the address for your prospective employer on the cover letter, follow it up with the purpose of the letter clearly written in capital letters.

Remember that the preferred font to use when presenting your resume is New Times Roman. It is not appropriate to use other flashy fonts because they look good and improve on the general presentation of your resume. This is just an excuse for a prospective employer to move on to the next resume.

Prospective employers want to see professionally prepared documents that present information about you in an orderly manner. Do not include flashy things in the hope of improving the appearance of the resume. At the end of the day, what really counts is the information you have provided about yourself and your suitability for the role.

When preparing the resume, remember that it is better to keep it in a standard format and not indenting the paragraphs. It is better to present it as blocks rather than indenting the beginning of the paragraphs. This gives it the professional look that it needs and makes it easier for the prospective employer to go through.

Divide the document into three distinct sections; an introduction, body, and conclusion. The resume should first thank the prospective employer for the opportunity and give a brief introduction about yourself and what you are currently doing.

The body of the cover letter should provide a discussion of the main purpose of the resume. The conclusion should express the hope of working together with your prospective employer while the layout of the resume should begin with personal information, education history, work experience, and individual interests.

It is also possible to prepare a professional video resume that is even more straightforward than a printed resume. Depending with the instructions of each employer, you can prepare a short video presentation of yourself that strictly provides relevant information about your work history, education history, and experiences.

A professionally prepared video resume is equally effective in getting its main message across because the employer immediately familiarizes themselves with you and can assess you much more than from a printed piece of paper.

An employer will watch your video and take note of your own mannerisms before coming to a decision. It is necessary that you follow the same format of a resume when preparing the video resume to ensure that you provide as much relevant information as possible to your prospective employer.

In the video, begin by sharing personal information such as your name, your age and your marital status. Swiftly move into your education history, highlighting your primary school, secondary school and the universities that you have attended.

When you finally get a response from a prospective employer, they are likely to ask you for an interview in order to learn more about you. It is important that you have specific interview skills that will help you get past the challenges of convincing your prospective employer from the get-go.

When conducting an interview, it is more likely that you will do it via Skype or any popular video conferencing platform. This will allow you to speak to a prospective client directly regardless of where you are in the world and you will have to follow the general specification of normal interviews.

One of the most important skills that you need to have when speaking in an interview is coherence. It is absolutely important that you can speak in a straightforward manner, using simple language so that your prospective employer is left in no doubt about what you are talking about.

Coherence can make all the difference when you are addressing a prospective employer because they will have no use for somebody who cannot present themselves well. Make sure you speak simplistically but keeping in line with the need to be formal in your approach.

You have to be very patient when conducting an interview because you are answerable to your interviewer. If they want to take their time and speak to you about things you might feel are unrelated, be patient enough to answer their questions and even engage them.

Always ensure that you create enough time to conduct an interview and that you have nothing else distracting you. Patience makes all the difference because prospective employers want employees who are easy to speak to and respectable of basic tenets of courtesy.

Another important thing that you must keep in mind is that being in a good mood changes everything. A prospective employer does not want to hire somebody who is constantly moody or not willing to interact much because they are afraid that it will be the norm once they get hired.

As much as it is a tense situation for you, try to smile and look lively. Be happy about the opportunity not just in writing, but in speech, facial expressions, and body language, as well. Being in good mood changes so much and it makes the person interviewing you feel more at ease with you.

When you are conducting your interview on Skype, put the laptop computer on a flat surface, preferably a table and take a sit right in front of the camera. It is necessary for you to sit upright in a well lit room so that there are no visual problems for your interviewer.

Do not pace about the room or constantly change your position during the interview. If anything, if you can remain still for the duration of the interview and minimize your movements, you will be able to conduct a successful one. However, if you have to move about, specifically request permission from your interviewer before doing so.

Make sure that you keep time when setting up for your interview. If your interviewer tells you that the interview will start at nine o'clock, then be ready ten minutes prior to this deadline. Make sure you log into Skype or the relevant platform well before the appointed time.

Most remote jobs hinge on timely delivery of work, and so if you cannot guarantee that you can keep an interview on time, then there is no guarantee that you will be completing your work on time. Do not be late at any costs and if you feel that you will be, warn your interviewer well in advance.

Do not be quiet and restrict yourself to answering only the questions that the interviewer presents to you. It is necessary for you to be interactive and show your interest in the job by speaking about it and even asking questions especially if there is something you do not understand.

An interviewer will be interested in somebody who is ready to speak and be interactive, and if possible, provide even more relevant information than you have already presented in your resume. A successful interview is conducted by somebody willing to share information and be inquisitive.

Remember that as much as it is necessary to interact with your interviewer, always be honest when addressing them. Do not present fictitious information when speaking to an interviewer because they have the capability of confirming everything you say.

You might think that because it is a remote job, it is no problem lying about some experience you have attained. You might want to impress your interviewer by highlighting past organizations you have worked for when this is clearly not the case.

If you do this and you interviewer is able to confirm that it is a lie, you lose your credibility immediately. Be honest because even interviewers will appreciate an inexperienced prospective worker who is ready to learn and work hard.

When your interviewer is presenting themselves, they are likely to state a title or reference to a position they hold at the company. Out of respect, keep in mind such a title when addressing them because it can make all the difference when seeking to land a job.

A respectful approach to your interviewer is the only ticket to a job opportunity in their enterprise. If your interviewer tells you that they are a professor, address them as such instead of referring them to 'mister' or 'madam.' It is far much better to use their titles when speaking with them.

Always be ready to provide relevant examples when you are speaking directly with your interviewer. Examples help to show your experience and they also help to validate everything you are saying. It helps bring to life some of the projects you have worked on in the past.

Examples are a key part of the interview because most job seekers assume by simply stating that they have the experience, they can get away with it. In line with being honest, do not make up stories about work you have one in the past when in reality it is not true because your prospective employer will be able to spot this immediately.

Throughout the conversation with your interviewer, be sure to make eye contact with them throughout and display confidence in both your appearance and your voice. Do not let your eyes dart around the room aimlessly because it will also affect your concentration.

Your interviewer wants to see that you are a competent and trustworthy person, and maintaining eye contact particularly when they ask questions will help them feel at ease with you. Make sure that they can keep track of your own reactions by fully concentrating on everything they say.

Always remember to be very thankful right at the end of the interview. Most people do not take this point very seriously because the interviewer is offering you an opportunity to quit your desk job and start working remotely.

Understand the importance of the situation and be sure to state your gratefulness at the impending opportunity. You must leave your interviewer thinking very positively about you right to the last and this will ensure that they will be giving you a ring sooner rather than later.

Depending on the nature of the job, some interviewers might opt to conduct their interviews over the phone. This might be a more straightforward approach for them, but there are also some mannerisms you should consider in such a situation.

First, make sure that your location is somewhere you can speak without interruptions in network service. It might be possible that your current location is not receptive of phone signals, and this might speak volumes to an interviewer looking to employ you in their organization.

Make sure that you raise your voice and speak audibly the entire time so that your interviewer is left in no doubt about what you are talking about. Being loud and clear is important in ensuring that there is no confusion with what you are saying during the duration of the interview.

Do not speak meekly and make your interviewer constantly ask you to speak louder. This will immediately put them off and they will easily end the interview as a result. Make sure than when you are having this conversation, be in a place where you can speak audibly without too much noise around you.

Even if you are speaking into a phone, leave your interviewer in no doubt that you are eagerly looking forward to having the job. Show your enthusiasm just from the tone of your voice and the manner in which you address them because it will make all the difference when they are considering you for the job.

Enthusiasm is a crucial part of a successful interview because interviewers want prospective employees who are eager to work for them and contribute to the success of the organization. If your voice shows that you are quite happy and privileged to be speaking to them, they will invite you to work for them.

Be sure to ask for the interviewer's name and/or title at the beginning of the interview, and make sure you address them as such throughout. Do not make empty responses and show your obviousness that you have no idea who you are speaking to because it is not a good sign.

You must display high courtesy levels and let it be known to your interviewer that you are an outgoing person. Address them in a direct manner as it will make them feel comfortable and even familiar with you, and such subtle hints will guide you towards your dream remote job.

When your interviewer asks you something over the phone, be quick to respond and do not make them wait for too long before you share your response. Be precise with them when sharing information and try your best to keep up with everything they are saying.

Do not delay your responses particularly when they ask you something direct about yourself. A delayed response can be a possibility of you thinking of something appropriate to say instead of just speaking the truth. Do not leave your conversations hanging for too long because it is likely that the interviewer has other people to interview.

Be a very keen listener even if it is necessary to be interactive when having a conversation with your interviewer. If you are too quick to speak even before letting them finish a sentence, your interviewer will feel it appropriate not to speak to you further.

Listen keenly to what they have to say also because they might present you with new information necessary to ensure the interview succeeds. Whatever the interviewer speaks, pay close attention because they might tell you something you did not expect.

If necessary, be prepared with a script that will guide you on the most appropriate ways of answering the interviewer's questions. Have a sheet of paper prepared that highlights different types of questions you are likely to respond to and how best to structure your answers.

You will be surprised that a chit sheet can make all the difference when conducting an interview over the phone. The advantage is that you will not have the interviewer seeing that you are referring to a chit sheet, but they will be able to keep up with your responses easily.

Be interactive throughout the telephone conversations and be sure to ask lots of questions. Do not hang and let the interviewer speak almost by themselves, constantly having to ask you if you are still on the line. Be lively when having the conversation as this will make all the difference with the way your interviewer will portray you.

Section 2
Chapter 4: Time Management

In a remote job, everything is different particularly if you are used to the routine of a desk job.

You have to manage your time wisely unlike in an office environment where your boss is in control of how time is spent in the office. When you are working under somebody in a desk job, you want to waste as much time as possible so that you can go home sooner rather than later.

With a remote job, however, it is vital to manage your own time and keep yourself at work for as long as possible. You will be surprised y these parallels because nobody will push you to work when you are at home but yourself.

It can be a challenging task managing time effectively because when somebody is at home, all they want to do is relax and take it easy. Working remotely presents the unique challenge of managing time effectively because it is the only way of ensuring you complete your projects on time.

Take note that when working for an employer remotely, they have great expectations on you. They expect you to be able to deliver quality work on time and in a consistent manner. This is the most effective way of establishing credibility with your employer and working for them long term.

There are many freelancers who do not understand that time management is the most important aspect of remote work. As appealing as it might sound, if you have gotten used to a desk job, you will find it very difficult to cope working at home when expectations are high on you.

In this respect, you have to come up with effective time management skills that allow you to complete projects in a timely manner. There are a number of important things that you must consider when working remotely so as to ensure that you efficiently manage your time.

First, you must set your working hours and know the most appropriate time for you to start and finish your work. It is necessary to work within a given time frame everyday particularly when it is quiet and convenient for you to put in a shift.

When you set your hours for work, it becomes difficult to deviate from working during this time period. Deep down, you will know that if you do not work at a certain time, you will not be able to get the work done at any other time and consequently, you will miss an important deadline.

You also need to prepare your work space in advance so that when you start working, you do not get distracted by basic preparations. Make sure you have a specific corner or desk wherever you will work remotely that is free and available for you during your working hours.

Preparing where to work in advance helps to save a lot of time because if you keep doing the practice during working hours, you will not be able to get as much work done as possible within a day. You have to prepare everything you will need for work before actually putting in a shift.

Planning your day in advance is equally important because you need to know exactly what you have to complete within a given time frame in order to complete your given tasks. Prepare for the next day in advance because you will be amazed by how smoothly everything will go.

Have a picture in your head about how you want to spend the following day; imagine yourself working at your desk or work station, handling different challenges and tasks. Visualize the work you will actually have to do and understand the need to prepare for it in advance.

When you plan for your day, take into consideration any other obligations that you have. If you have other house chores that you need to complete, make a decision whether to suspend such duties; if you have a guest who is visiting, consider rescheduling.

You can also write down what you will need to do the following day, and this will be instrumental in helping you manage your time. There is no need to manage your time for the day when it already begins because you are already spending precious time that you do not have.

Remember that all work and no play makes Jack a very dull boy. If you truly want to succeed in working remotely and managing your time effectively, then you must set aside enough time to take a breather and rest from all the work that you have to do.

Rest is just as important as hard work because you will burn out particularly if you are working consistently and settled into a routine. When you burn out, it becomes very hard to maintain your concentration and put in the same amount of work you would within an hour.

Planning in advance time to rest is important because if you continuously work, you will not realize when you are starting to slack off in your work. You will start sleeping right on your desk during working hours because you are so exhausted and your eyes are even in pain.

Proper rest keeps the mind and body active and you can achieve this sense of freshness every day. Be sure to spend adequate amounts of time sleeping and minimize the amount of time you socialize with other people because they can intrude into time meant exclusively for rest.

You should be wary of visitors and friends who will want to visit you when you are working. It might be that your working hours is the time when all your friends are free, and they will want to come over and visit, hang out and even go out for a meal.

This can be very frustrating for you particularly if you have difficult deadlines to meet and your boss is waiting for you. It is almost impossible to work with the distraction posed by a friend and it is appropriate to ensure that you have no visitors during hours when you really should be working.

Manage the time you spend with your friends because it is the only sure way of working at the appropriate hours. When you have your friends in check, you can be sure of putting in work with minimal distractions because it wastes precious time that you do not have.

There is nothing wrong with meeting your friends but try and restrict such meetings to the end of the day. If you start meeting up with your friends early in the day, chances are they will deviate you from what you need to do, resulting in you wasting lots of time.

You should also be wary of the things that waste your time when you are working. Understand your own flaws so that you can improve your working culture. You will realize that there are several small things that you will not notice at first, but they consume a lot of your time.

If you find yourself spending too much time in front of a screen during meal times, you will discover that you could put to use a significant amount of time doing something much more useful. During working days, make sure entertainment takes no priority in your hierarchy of responsibilities.

There are several other small things that consume a significant amount of time that when you combine, you will realize you are losing several hours a day. It is necessary to identify the causes of some of the time wasters in your life so that you can reduce the amount of time on these extracurricular activities.

Time wasting sometimes happens subconsciously because you do not realize that what you are doing is not particularly productive. It can be spending that extra thirty minutes in bed after your alarm clock has gone off, but that is three and a half hours you are losing every week just like that.

You should always have a long term plan of what you want to achieve when you start working remotely and some of the ambitions you intend to achieve. A long term plan is a critical necessity for any remote worker because it provides them the motivation to sit at their workplace every day and be productive.

A long term plan should begin by identifying the reason you are leaving your daytime desk job for a remote position. It is necessary to understand yourself and your own motivations for working in a different environment that will change your life permanently.

You need to identify some of the problems you intend to solve by working remotely, such as making more money, achieving better comfort in your life and starting the path of entrepreneurship. Whatever your intentions are, plan for them as this will enable you to have a picture of the amount of work you must complete each day.

A good solid plan should identify the essence of proper time management because it will allow you to establish discipline within yourself. You will know that you have a certain amount of work to complete every day and this target must be achieved by all means necessary.

Another small aspect of proper time management that you might underestimate but is extremely crucial is ensuring that your phone and laptop computer are constantly charged. There is nothing more annoying than waking up to start working only to realize that your batteries are flat out.

There are many people who have missed important deadlines, skipped life-changing interviews and missed out on important information simply because the phone or laptop was not charged. As small a problem as it might seem, it is capable of completely turning your day around.

If you are used to going to the office on a daily basis, it might take some time for you to get used to the routine of reliably charging your laptop every day. It is a habit that you must develop and ensure it sticks with you because it is the most effective way of managing your time.

Do not miss out on important phone calls simply because your batteries have run out. When you start working remotely, you will soon realize that what initially seemed like no problem is suddenly an important part of your life and capable of determining if you keep your job.

You also need to learn the most effective way of dealing with inconveniences because they are bound to happen. It is almost impossible to have a continuous week where there were barely any external distractions that have caused you to slow down on your normal work output.

Inconveniences come in many shapes and sizes, but you must always be prepared. One of the most effective things to do to prepare for inconveniences is visualizing them happening when you are trying to complete important tasks. If you can foresee an inconvenience, you will be in a better position to mitigate the risk it pauses.

One of the major inconveniences that affect people when they are working remotely is noise making. If you are working out of a coffee shop, for example, and a group of people walk in speaking and laughing very loudly, it is unlikely that you will concentrate properly.

The solution to this is wearing earphones and playing soft music or even rain sounds. If you can drown the distraction posed by noise within your vicinity with this simple strategy, you can handle other small inconveniences that can cause you to delay your work.

It is very important to have a clear mind when you start working remotely because you must set the intended goals you want to achieve. The best thing for you is to write them down and visualize yourself actually achieving these goals as a result of your hard work.

Ask yourself this; what is the objective of this remote job, do I just want to be comfortable or do I want to completely change my life? When you set goals, keep in mind factors such as making more money, achieving independence in your life and learning new skills.

The goals that you set will be influential in determining how hard you work in your newfound remote job. Your work productivity will be influenced almost exclusively by your desire to achieve your goals and move into a completely new way of living.

Do not be afraid to be ambitious as this will only guarantee that you will put in hard work whenever you are at your remote job. Ambitious plans will prompt you onwards and you will be in a position to start becoming happy as long as you work consistently.

Whenever you are mapping out your responsibility as you begin your remote work, remember that it is important to address what is important first rather than what is urgent. There is a fine distinction between the two terms and every good remote worker needs to understand this in order to succeed.

Important responsibilities can include completing work that will contribute to your overall invoice for a particular financial period, convincing a client to work with you because of the promise of long term business and finding a market for your work before you begin.

Urgent work that you might have to complete most likely aligns with a deadline that s fast approaching. If you promise a customer the completion of a project by a specific time, it becomes an urgent task because you have to ensure you deliver just as you promised.

However, in such a situation where you have to choose between finishing the important job first or the urgent one, always select to complete the important job first. This is the best way forward because important work will define the entire structure of your remote job.

Learn how to keep yourself motivated on off-days when you are resting as this is key to success. Whenever you find yourself with some extra time, focus on resting but also think of your responsibilities in a light way. You do not have to solve any challenges at that point but keep in mind that you have a good job.

Most remote workers do not have many problems motivating themselves particularly if they have already set goals. But the key to motivating yourself when you are not working is to ensure that you do not lose interest in your work or come up with a different way of completing your tasks.

One of the best ways of keeping motivated when on an off-day is engaging in entertaining things that will build on the progress you have already made. For instance, playing general-knowledge games is an excellent way of keeping the brain fresh while at the same time relaxing from a strenuous schedule.

When you remain motivated, you will be positive about the upcoming challenges you have to face. Similarly, you can completely get your mind off the tasks that are awaiting you to give yourself a chance for maximum rest so that when you wake up, you can handle your responsibilities easily.

It is very important to understand the essence of concentration when you are working at a remote job and trying to manage your time. When you are not concentrating fully at work, it is difficult to achieve any success in your endeavors because your mind is not there.

Maintain concentration by warding off thoughts that distract you from the task in hand. Keep in mind that you have a schedule to follow and drown out external distractions that will affect your concentration. The more you concentrate, the more work you can o within a given time period.

You need to set aside specific time for handling chores and you must ensure that they do not intrude with your normal working schedule. There are remote workers who underestimate the importance of a schedule for their chores and other house responsibilities that it sometimes infringes on their normal working hours.

When you have a definite time for handling your chores, you guarantee that there will be minimal distractions when you are completing your responsibilities. It is necessary to ensure that your normal house work does not interrupt your remote work because, in this situation, one is important while the other is urgent.

The most successful remote workers do not wake up during normal working hours like the rest of the working population. Instead, they get an early morning such that by the time the day is beginning in earnest, they have already done a large percentage of their daily work.

Waking up early should be a staunch principle for any remote worker who is looking to complete a large volume of work each day. The early bird truly catches the worm and this characterizes remote workers who never miss out on deadlines and are very strict with their time management techniques.

You should also take some time to pretend that your remote work space is your office. If you can visualize your own life having to report to a desk every morning, transfer those thoughts to your remote workspace and think of it as your office in the same sense.

This will provide you with the extra motivation that you need to pursue your responsibilities and complete your work appropriately. You will be able to employ the same levels of seriousness as you do when working an office job because you will be conscious that it is an income earner for you, as well.

Do not restrict yourself to a single location whenever you are striving to manage your remote working time. You do not always have to do your work at home because you might become used to certain routines that consume your time needlessly.

There is also the possibility of unavoidable distractions when working from home, so consider spending some time in your local coffee shop or even the library for a change of environment. You will find that this simple technique makes all the difference with regard to how you manage your time.

If you want to manage your time effectively while working in a remote job, consider minimizing the amount of time you watch TV and even chat with your friends on social media. These two forms of media are the most distractive types for remote workers and they can render them jobless within a short time.

Be wary of the communication to your friends that you have become reliant on because it will influence the amount of work you can do. It is not wise to deceive yourself that you are working hard and need a television break because this will waste more time than you have available.

Make sure that you understand yourself well and that you can tell what your most productive hours are. This is vital because you need to ensure that you put in work when your mind is at its freshest. There is no better work you can do than during your most productive hours.

For most remote workers, the most productive times they can work is the early morning hours when it is still quiet and everybody is still in bed. After coming off a night's sleep, the mind is very ready to handle different responsibilities and might be the most productive hours for remote workers.

Another serious distortion that affects several remote workers is daydreaming. It is very hard to restrict your mind from wandering particularly when you are working alone in silence and thinking about many things at the same time. Sometimes the mind just wanders off without you even noticing.

If this should happen, you should find a way of keeping your concentration such as switching on the television in the background but maintaining the volume at its lowest levels. Bring yourself back to your work because daydreaming is such a time consuming exercise that it distracts you from what you really need to be doing.

It is essential to communicate your intentions with anybody that you live with and even your friends so that they can understand the changes t your lifestyle. You will constantly get interrupted by the people around you if you do not let them know your intentions, and this will waste a lot of precious time that you already do not have.

If you live with your family, let them know what you are doing and the importance of supporting the remote job in any way possible. When you communicate your intentions with those around you, they will be mindful of your time and ensure that they do not waste it in any way.

Most people who work remote jobs maintain time management applications that enable them to manage their time effectively. These applications are several all over the internet and any prospective remote worker will be spoilt for choice when settling for one.

Each time management application has its own unique features and you should take your time to go through them to determine what works best for you. Each application is geared towards different personalities of people because they have different specifications and they help in ensuring that you do not waste any time at all during your working days.

There are several time management apps that you can choose from, but you should make your choices depending on your schedule and the nature of the job that you are handling. It is easy to find the most effective application for your use because there are numerous of them to choose from.

One of the more reliable applications that is free and available for both iOS applications and Mac is Be Focused Timer. This is a useful application because it helps you keep track of several responsibilities at once and even shows you your working history.

It is an excellent way of understanding what has to be completed and any pending work that you require. It has an alarm that goes off at different points to indicate the grouping of responsibilities that you must deal with in a given time frame.

With this application, you can even set aside time for a break, and it offers encouraging messages that help you relax and keep time. It is an excellent way of keeping up with a lot of work when you have a lot of responsibilities to handle in a single day, and it helps you maximize your productivity.

Another useful application that can help you manage your time is the Loop-Habit Tracker. This application is available for Android devices and it helps you avoid distractive behaviors that waste your time everyday and cause you not to meet your deadlines.

The application makes you respond to various functions that you have to repeat on a daily basis to get rid of distracting behaviors that cost you time. There are dozens of specifications on the application that allow you to set alarms for different responsibilities and develop a productive routine.

Noisli is yet another useful application that is free when you use it on your computer but charges a fee of $1.99 for the application version. It is mainly a web application that you can easily access online and it is a useful time management application that is used by many remote workers.

This application is quite advantageous because it provides good background noise that drowns out other distractions that might be around you. There are custom mixes of noises including ocean waves and nature sounds that keep you completely focused when working.

Remember the Milk is yet another time management application whose basic version is free but requires a $39.99 fee paid yearly to access its pro features. This application allows for the creation of a comprehensive to-do list that allows you to complete your work in a timely manner.

The application is also known for sending reminders via email, messaging or through other applications It is an excellent way of keeping track with the list of things you must complete within a given time frame and it keeps you in line to ensure all uncompleted work is tended to.

Todoist is another popular application among freelancers but it costs $4 for every month for its premium version while it costs $5 for its business version. The billings are done annually for both versions and they are available for iOS, Android and desktop versions.

This application is an excellent tool to assist you as a remote worker to manage time because it improves your task management. It has several features that allow you to complete your tasks according to the set deadlines, and it even lets you achieve 'karma points' for the task you complete consistently and on time.

The Focus Booster application is another time management tool that helps you track your work and link different projects you are working on. It is useful because it gives you an overall assessment of your work and emphasizes the individual activities you need to complete to handle an entire briefcase of responsibilities.

This application is free upon downloading but you will have to pay $2.99 a month after the first thirty days. The professional version of this application will cost you $4.99 a month and it is available for iOS, Android devises as well as a desktop version.

The Kiwake Alarm Clock is also another useful time management application that brings a whole new meaning to alarm clocks. When it sets off, the only way you can switch out the noise and clanging sounds is by getting to it and playing a brain game that shuts down the alarm when you get it right.

It is the perfect application if you have trouble getting out of sleep, and it will put you straight into the mood to work. The application costs $7.99 and is available only on iOS. Choosing this as a time management tool will ensure that you are always alert and on your feet.

The Focus@Will application is also an important time management application that hosts a different collection of music suitable for a quiet working environment. This application was developed by neuroscientists and it is specific for putting you in the most relaxed mood possible so that you maintain your concentration while at your remote job.

The application is billed in terms of its users, with two to five users paying $9.95 every month, six to fifty users paying $8.95 every month, fifty one to one hundred and fifty users paying $6.95 and 151 to 250 users paying $4.95 a month. It is available for iOS and android devices.

If you want to block out websites and other applications that are constantly interrupting you while you are working, consider the time management application called Freedom. This application helps you customize your work sessions so that other distractions, such as social media messages only reach you after your set working hours.

This is a useful application for those who are threatened by constant interruptions every day, and the pricing options are either $6.99 per month or a one-off annual fee of $129. This application is available for Mac, iOS and Windows.

OmniFocus is another useful application that helps you manage your time while at your remote job by providing a calendar-view of your tasks. It is possible to manage different times for each project by setting a timer, and it is particularly useful for syncing data while at work.

The application costs a standard fee of $39.99 but you can purchase the pro version for

$79.99. The application is available for both Mac and iOS and it is particularly useful for those looking to save up on extra time and keeping up with a tight schedule consisting of several tasks.

The Forest App is a cheap option for those looking for a convenient application to assist them to manage their time. Remote workers usually have to part with $1.99 for access to this application, and it is available for iOS and Android applications.

The application helps you to creatively maintain your concentration by planting a forest on the application's screen an encouraging you on. The trees start to wither when your concentration dips or you stop working and it will give you a polite reminder of the tasks that lay ahead.

Chapter 5: Teamwork and Communication

Depending on the remote job you land, you will find that it is important for you to work in a team. The simple fact is any remote job that you land is a team work job because you have to liaise with one or more people in order to successfully complete your tasks.

Working as a team is the most effective way of achieving success because there are many people to help tackle a problem. It is always better to have assistance when solving different problems and team work more often than not results in success.

In order to work efficiently in a team, there are a number of best practices that you have to keep in mind in order to achieve the success you are after. When you start working full time on remote jobs, you will discover that teamwork becomes more important than ever because your own results will partly be based on the contributions of others.

One of the most important practices that ensure good team work even with people you have never met before is identifying the perfect leadership for the group. It is necessary for all members of the group to settle on a single individual who will be responsible for organizing the group and representing every single member.

A good team communicates regularly with each other to give status updates and to share new ideas. This is quite important because communication provides a link to each team member and ensures everybody is on the same page with regard to the ambitions of the group.

Efficient communication is one of the basic elements of good team work as it brings the members of the group together in an effective manner. When you are able to share ideas easily and speak freely to one another, it becomes easier to work and handle your responsibilities.

Another best practice that ensures remote workers can work efficiently as a team is engaged in team building exercises. Even though there is a massive amount of distance separating the group members, this does not mean that they cannot interact together to strengthen the bond of the group.

Playing online games together and having an opportunity to chat, for example on a Whatsapp group enables close ties to be developed among group members. This is extremely important particularly for group members who rarely meet each other as they will need activities that bring them closer together.

It is essential to have strict team rules that everybody abides by, starting with the leader of the group. When you set identifiable rules for each group member, they understand their obligation to one another and it sets the tone for the type of structure that the group will maintain.

Setting rules are particularly important because remote workers might sometimes want to make decisions and take matters into their own hands. When there is an identified structure for the group to coordinate through, it becomes easier for everybody to work remotely without much hindrance.

When the team is being created, the only way remote workers will be able to work in a coordinated fashion is if the objectives of the union are clearly identified from the get-go. There is no group that can successfully achieve its objectives if they have not been spelt out in the first place.

All group members must make a contribution to this, stating the objective that they feel necessary for everybody to follow. It is upon the group leader to validate the objectives that reflect the efforts of the entire group, and it should be feasible and achievable or each member.

It is very important to recognize and reward the efforts of each group member because it is a source of motivation in itself. When you get congratulated by a member of the group for a job well done, you feel nice and want to contribute much more to the progress of the group.

Identifying each individual accomplishments of the group members will serve as an example for the rest of the group members. They will be able to emulate this example that has been set and create a standard for the other group members to meet. This ensures that work is done efficiently.

There should be adequate space for everybody to work in even when the workers are remote. If you have a common working platform, everybody should be accorded enough space to allow them to store their content as well as the progress of their work.

If the entire group is using a single email address for sending work, for example, everybody should be allocated adequate hard disk space so as to make contributions without a problem. This is the role of the leader and he must ensure that everybody is able to work on level terms without any preferential treatment.

It is important to take breaks together and not have a single member of the group hard at work when everybody else is resting. It is necessary to try and reflect each other's schedules to try as much as possible to work in real time so as to share information more easily.

When going on breaks, be sure that every other group member has completed their portion of work so that you are all able to work simultaneously. It is not fair for one of you to be resting while the rest of you are hard at work; a proper group should take into consideration the input of every individual comprising it.

You should spend some time identifying the strengths of each group member and focusing on them because it is these key contributions that will result in success as a group. It might be difficult to identify the strengths of other group members when working remotely, but it is possible to identify them from their work.

You might find that there are group members who are very quick at typing while there are others who are very good at composing stories. If your group consists of writers, divide up the responsibilities such that each person specializes in their main strengths when working together.

Be sure to show gratitude when working in a group because appreciating every individual effort will make all the difference in the completion of different tasks. Do not let the good work of a group member go unrecognized because they will also sow their gratitude when you make a significant contribution.

Gratitude is another way of expressing the direction that the group is heading, and it also shows a sense of dedication from the group members. When you show gratitude, you create a gracious working environment even though all of you are working remotely.

It is necessary to accept the fact that not all of you can be the same within the group. There is bound to be some differences among you even if you are working on the same project within a similar industry. It is necessary to appreciate the skills of each individual member of the group.

The functioning of the group is in fact guided by the differences displayed by every member. The fact that you are not all the same means that you can contribute in an appropriate manner to ensure the objectives of the group are met by focusing on your strengths.

Despite the distance separating group members when working remotely, it is possible to celebrate when you hit various milestones. Celebrating as a group is essential in creating a strong team spirit because it shows a high level of dedication among each member.

There are various ways of celebrating long distance, such as having a lengthy video call conference where everybody is given a chance to speak out. It is also possible to celebrate by paying each other in a pre-agreed way such that every member of the group feels the benefit.

Remember that a professional group is not so different from a social group because the values of trust and respect still apply to significant effect. All group members must learn to accept and understand the differences that exist among everybody and be culturally educated.

When there is respect among group members, work can be done with greater efficiency because everybody is working to each other's strengths to achieve pre-determined objectives. A group that lacks basic respect for each other will soon crumble and it will be impossible to do any remote work.

Group work also thrives when the values of commitment to each other are strictly observed. All group members must remain committed to the set objectives and only alter their cause if there is an accepted change to the objectives. A proper group functions because everybody is moving in one direction.

Commitment means that each group member is available to chat at pre-designated times, ready to do extra work if need be and ready to offer another group member a hand when things get really challenging. There should be no member of the group who wants to do things differently from the rest because this is the beginning of them acting independently.

Remember that a good group displays signs of adaptability because it is necessary for each group member to adapt to the new working situation. This is a strict requirement for remote jobs because you might have to work from anywhere depending on the levels of distractions in your immediate surroundings.

A remote worker will be unable to work in a group if they are not adaptable to changes in the functioning of the group. Changes are bound to happen and every group member must be flexible and responsive when new methods of working and achieving the objectives are introduced.

Another best practice when working in teams is ensuring that there is creative freedom for all group members when pursuing the group's objectives. There is nothing more important than allowing group members to speak out their minds because this is the basis of most ideas that will drive the group forward.

Creativity is an important aspect of achieving success when working remotely because sometimes, you just have to think outside the box. When group members are creative, they will constantly be interacting with each other because of the abundance of ideas and ways of circumventing risks.

Make sure that there is a deep sense of positivity in the group by minimizing complaints and looking to satisfy the individual needs of every group member. It is inappropriate for group members to gang up on one of them in an effort to make them avoid doing something that they feel is right.

For instance, if one of the group members wants to introduce prayers before everybody starts working, there is no reason to refuse. Such activity will create positivity and should be encouraged because it makes working as a group exciting as everybody develops a close bond with each other.

A proper functioning group solves problems rather than letting them drag out for long durations of time and creating massive disharmony in the group. If there are common problems being experienced by the group members or even just one of you, you should all sit and discuss collectively.

An efficient group is always able to find its way around common problems that might otherwise cripple the functioning of the group. If there are any issues threatening the progress that has already been achieved by the group, the rules that have been set as well as good leadership should be the source of a solution.

If a group can adequately solve problems, it is a display of best practices and sets an example for other remote workers. An efficient group should not only come up with viable solutions but those that can solve pre-existing problems over a long term basis.

The presentation of viable solutions is an essential element of efficient group work because it shows the closeness established by the individual members of the group. This is ironic because everybody is working remotely but still able to agree on basic ways of ensuring progress within.

Group work is all about equality even if there is a group leader and all the participants are working remotely. Everybody should be given a fair share of the work, a chance to speak and contribute ideas as well as hosting different forums within the group.

Fairness is another basic tenet of a successful group that makes the distance separating the members irrelevant. A goo group is able to achieve success on the basis of equal sharing so that nobody is overburdened by excessive work or nobody is overlooked as the entire group looks to achieve its objectives.

It is also important to note that a good group represents a fair sense of diversity even if each of you is working in the same industry. If you are a group of writers with the objective of completing a book together, you have to maximize the diverse experiences of each of you.

Among a group of writers, there is likely to be a typist, a person in charge of creativity, an editor an even a publisher. When everybody works to their strengths owing to the diversity of their skills, it makes achieving group objectives much easier because nobody has to handle responsibilities that they are not familiar with.

An excellent group that intends to achieve success working remotely displays excellent organization as an element of best practice. This is primarily the responsibility of the leader and they must ensure that there is no confusion when members of the group are working.

It is quite irritating to work for a group that has no organization because it is possible for two group members to do the same thing at the same time, thereby wasting time. If there is an organization in a group of web designers, each person will be responsible for different aspects of the job that they are specialist in.

It is important for group members to have fun as they work together as this strengthens the bonds that already exist. A boring group will find it difficult to achieve success because some members will even stop concentrating and paying as much attention as they should.

It is possible to engage in small talk while the entire group works because it is relaxing and can cut the tension that exists. Group members will feel less pressured and prompted to work harder if there is a sense of fun among group members and excitement at their responsibilities.

In case the group experiences a stand-off where a suggestion is threatening to break apart the group, consider settling the issue with a vote. This is a good way for the group to express itself and a majority vote will help release group members from any deadlock affecting their work.

A vote is a simple and straightforward approach to handling problems that will threaten the continuation of group activities. It is a good way of solving problems that are particularly serious because it gives a chance for every group member to express their opinion with regard to the functioning of the group.

If you want to improve your own work while working n a group and even if you are working remotely, one of the most efficient ways is to analyze the work of other group members. It is possible to emulate the good work completed by another group member as a source of guidance.

Examine the approaches being made by some of the other group members because this is the whole point of being in a group. Do not be afraid to be inquisitive if there is something you do not understand because other group members will graciously come to your assistance.

As much as the best practices are appropriate for ensuring group success, it is also necessary to establish appropriate ways of communicating as group members. There is a different approach to communication when working remotely and is a stark difference to the level of communication inside offices.

One of the more important things to observe when looking to communicate efficiently and effectively in the group is to have open meetings. This can be achieved through video phone calls where everybody in the group is present and emulates an actual meeting in an office.

An open meeting should be hosted by the group leader and they will be responsible for sharing links to the video call. No single group member should ever be left out because they all have to contribute towards making the group function efficiently to achieve its objectives.

In an open meeting, every group member should be given an equal opportunity to communicate and air out any issues they might have. This is important because the purpose of an open meeting is to ensure that everybody can express their views to ensure that there is no weak link in the group.

Another effective and quick way of achieving communication in the group is by way of sending emails. These messages are usually instant and they ensure that each group member receives vital information in real time. Emails allow for the transmission of information in an appropriate way as you can send documents, video and even audio recordings.

The other advantage of using emails for remote workers working as a group is that it is cheap. Emails do not cost anything depending on the service provider, and all each group member will need is a stable internet connection as well as a reliable laptop computer.

As much as you are all working as a group, it is not a must that you all communicate together at the same time. If one group member needs assistance from another, they can liaise together and help each other achieve their individual objectives that contribute to the overall success of the group.

Understand the importance of engaging in one-on-one conversations with other group members as it develops a stronger bond between the two of you. One-on-one conversations help to align the objectives of different group members into one to guarantee that there is a strong sense of unity.

The most effective way of communicating while you are in groups is by creating a receptive atmosphere that encourages everybody to speak. The only way a group will function properly when it is comprised of remote workers is if there is a forum where everybody can express themselves freely.

It is important to have a receptive environment because each group member deserves to be heard. When you facilitate a receptive environment, your group colleagues will also create one for you whenever you have something important to share with everybody else.

Another way of ensuring the best approach to communication while working as a team is to express opinions during training. It is likely that all group members will have to refer to a common simulator or reference point to assist them in conducting their responsibilities.

This is the best time to communicate because you will be sharing each other's experiences as you learn new concepts. Sharing experiences in training brings out common problems being experienced by everybody as well as unique issues that have to be addressed to ensure that the group moves forward.

There is nothing more important than confidence when communicating because your team members will take you seriously. Even if you are asking a question but constantly displaying confidence and enthusiasm for working with everybody else, you will create stronger bonds with group members.

Since the remote work you are doing has now become your central income earner, group members will appreciate the seriousness shown by each person. It is necessary that you show your dedication to the common cause in the group as this is a source of motivation for everybody else.

As much as you might be taking your new position casually, you will find that there are group members whose livelihood is dependent on the remote work you are doing. It is necessary to be respectful to them and show that you are serious at all times and ready to make significant contributions to the group effort.

When communicating with fellow group members, keep in mind that adopting a simple way of communicating is the best way of spreading information. Even if you are all working in a similar industry, be careful about using complicated jargon that will make you difficult to understand.

Keep in mind that you want to be heard every time you talk and you want your opinions to count for something when handling different challenges. You will b able to achieve this if you avoid speaking in complicate terms and adopt a simplistic approach to chatting with other group members.

You should also consider using visuals and presentations when communicating with other group members. If you need to talk about complicate math, post statistics in the form of graphs and charts to a common message board to illustrate your points clearly.

Do not speak too much in a group when simplistic presentations are capable of expressing exactly what is in your head. Do not assume that group members will automatically understand you just because you have understood a difficult concept by yourself.

You should always be attentive and never be too quick to speak when one of the team members is speaking. It is a sign of respect to allow somebody else to finish what they are saying, particularly if they are addressing a group of people.

This is basic courtesy and it makes all the difference in determining the relationship among team members. Being a good listener offers you the chance to learn for yourself because you can observe different trends and have adequate time to prepare your answer.

Body language is also another form of communication that you can implement when having a conversation with group members. This will apply when you are having video conferences and all group members can see each other. Sometimes you will not have to speak much because your body movements are more audible.

Body posture and facial expressions also help, and it can be a courteous way to communicate especially if you want to interrupt one of your team members. Subtle body movements cannot be mistaken for a rude gesture particularly if you excuse yourself, and you will be able to communicate effectively.

The tone of your voice will also influence the effectiveness of your communication with fellow group members. If you genuinely want to share information within the group, use a low and friendly tone of voice, reserving the high-pitched approach to the leader of the group.

Always address your group members in a meek manner so as to encourage them to contribute, as well. Raising your voice sometimes discourages other group members to be engaged in conversation with you because they feel that there is a possibility of you being rude with them.

Avoid repetition when communicating with group members as this is particularly irritating if you are talking over the phone or on a video conference. You might feel that you need to emphasize a point and perhaps repeating it once is appropriate enough; however, repeating it over and over again is not appropriate.

Repetition can cause massive communication problems and confusion when trying to relay information to other group members. It becomes difficult to focus on the overall essence of the message if you choose to emphasize only one point. Since the success of the group is a collective effort, address each person with respect by avoiding constant repetition.

It is possible to create a work group profile on a social media platform that every group member can access. This forms an excellent mode of communication because it is possible to share large documents, images, audio and video files. A good working platform allows all of you to keep track of each other.

A group that is aiming to achieve similar objectives will find it very difficult to achieve success of they cannot rely on a single job board where they can post their messages to each other. It is also appropriate that such platforms support different types of files to make sharing amongst the group straightforward.

Remember that a little humor cannot hurt anyone if anything it is a best practice for communicating while in a group. Sometimes work can become very serious or everybody becomes stressed by the responsibilities they have to handle in a definite time period.

If you want to communicate effectively in such a situation, crack a joke, make a light moment with the rest of the team and distract them from their challenges for a minute. This will serve to change everything and it will make working together with all the more exciting.

Whenever you communicate, be sure to be articulate so that your team members are left in no doubt of what you are saying. Sometimes, in order to prove a point, there are people who will beat about the bush in an attempt to get everybody to be on the same page as them.

However, the simple fact remains that being clear about what you are communicating will endear you to your group members. As a group leader, you should always be articulate in your communication and considering all of you are remotely located, precise information is of absolute importance.

Never mumble when addressing group members because they will soon stop paying attention to you and even proceed with the affairs of the group without your help. Mumbling makes you inaudible particularly if you are speaking over a video conference or speaking over the phone.

Most people mumble and it is possible to get past this problem with some practice. If you are working remotely and in a group, practice having a conversation with yourself or a friend to try and get rid of the problem of stammering your words and failing to deliver your message clearly.

It is essential for you to remember that one of the best ways of communicating while in a group is to encourage feedback. Conversations among team members should always be a two-way street because everybody's contribution must be factored in when making important decisions.

It is not right to leave out anybody in the group especially when they have something to say. Give each other a chance to speak and listen to each other as this will improve communication even among a group of people who do not know each other. Communication is successful in a group when everybody has a voice.

When you communicate with fellow teammates, make sure to show your appreciation for any contribution they make towards the group. Any success they achieve is your success, as well because it is also helping you get one step closer to fulfilling your ambitions.

Remote work certainly becomes exciting when you can maintain contact with a group of people most likely located in different parts of the world. If you manage to maintain healthy communication channels between you, you are on the path to entrepreneurship and a successful future.

You should set time to communicate in a casual way away from work opportunities as a way of improving communication in a team. This can be achieved by all of you being in a similar Whatsapp group that allows all of you to chat and present interesting points of conversation as a way of relaxing.

When you are constantly in touch with each other, you have a good chance of improving communication means among each other. Also, when you chat casually, each group member is able to learn something new about the other person and it makes relating to them much simpler.

Communication can be achieved in a team of remote workers by utilizing work collaboration applications where it is also possible to keep track of the work other group members are doing.

You will be able to learn something from the completed work of other group members, and you will also be in a position to communicate with them directly when there is something you do not understand but is vital to the progress that the group is making.

There should be strict privacy rules that exist among team members to ensure that any communication between them does not filter out to the outside world. Each of you should respect each other's privacy and this single act will drastically improve the way you communicate with each other.

Chapter 6: Remote Work and Starting a Business

When you quit your desk job to start a remote job, you have already taken your first step to entrepreneurship.

It is interesting to note that 543,000 new people start businesses every month in the United States. Entrepreneurship is much more popular than you might believe and everybody seems to want a way out of their normal daytime desk jobs.

Very few people enjoy their current employment positions because they are not completely control of their own lives. When you work for other people, your life is partially controlled by them because there are a lot of things that you must be subservient to just to earn a living.

In the United States, there were roughly 28 million small

businesses by the turn of the decade. Of this number, 22 million businesses consist of self employed individuals who work for themselves. The trend of entrepreneurship has been on the increase because these numbers have effectively doubled presently.

There are subtle steps that you should follow when looking to start venturing into entrepreneurship, and getting a remote job is just the first part of the puzzle. Once you achieve independence by working for yourself, you will be able to come up with suitable business ideas.

The first step to achieving any success by transitioning from your daytime desk job to a remote job and eventually an entrepreneurial role is making a commitment. You must be prepared to sacrifice more than just money and resources in order to become a full fledged entrepreneur.

Most people do not like leaving their jobs until their business has picked up. This is an obvious business strategy because you do not want to leave a paying job and jump into a venture that is not profitable. It is wise to be patient first before quitting so that the business gains some ground.

Therefore, you should make a commitment in advance before stating your business venture as it is the only way you will be able to divide up your time. By committing yourself to entrepreneurship, your life will start changing progressively as you prepare for a new approach.

When you make a commitment, you vow to spend more time gathering information for your business and finding out the resources that you will need. It is necessary to start thinking like a businessman even if you are still employed so that if you change your mind, you will be able to understand your own preferences.

You should spend some time reflecting on your own strengths and weaknesses because it will help determine the direction you will be heading businesswise. Sit down and make a list of some of the things you consider your strengths and advantages for when you start running your business.

Some of the strengths you might possess include being good at math, having a strong interest in business or having strong language skills. Either way, whatever your strengths are, they will be responsible for guiding you through the important business decisions that you will have to make.

You should also take the time to identify your weaknesses because they are likely to slow down the progress you make in your business. It is difficult for most people to identify their own weaknesses because they might not want to acknowledge that they actually exist.

Some of the weaknesses you might have despite wanting to be an entrepreneur includes a lack of interest for business, poor interaction skills with other people and access to low finances. However, there are several entrepreneurs in the country today who literally started from nothing and are now running multimillion dollar companies.

The next step to entrepreneurship even when you are still at your daytime job is to validate the idea you have come up with. It is necessary to first confirm that you can actually achieve success with a definite business plan before proceeding only to realize that it is not viable.

There are a number of ways that you can validate a business plan and ensure that it is appropriate for your ambitions. The first way is by conducting interviews with close friends and even prospective customers if you have achieved some headway into the market.

Interviews are effective methods of getting the responses you require because everybody will be prompted to offer viable information that will result in you making a good decision. The advantage of interviews is that you can interact one-on-one with persons of interests and ask all relevant questions that will lead you to implementing your business idea.

Another way of validating business plans that will liaise with your remote work is creating prototypes that you can distribute for free. If you have a new, unique product but still unsure whether it will sell, give it out for free in the initial stages of setting up the business.

The responses of prospective customers will be instrumental in letting you know whether a specific product can achieve any success in the market. If customers purchase the prototype and ask for more, consider putting your business plan into motion and starting the business.

You can also conduct a survey and seek additional information from prospective customers about what they think of definite products and services. A survey allows you to ask specific questions that can be geared towards product and service development so as to ensure the introduction of a business that is actually relevant to the surrounding community.

The other way you can validate a business plan while still at work is by presenting the information on social media. This is an excellent forum because it allows people to give their opinions via comments and it will be possible to know the likeability of a product or service within a short time.

Social media will connect you with customers and business people from around the world. It is the right place to post pictures, videos or even audio recordings that articulate the product or service you are introducing. After validating a business idea, you should take the first steps into establishing an entrepreneurship venture.

Successful entrepreneurship consists of the entrepreneur introducing a good or service to the market that displays a competitive advantage over other products and services. This is another avenue for launching your entrepreneurial business because you will focus on products that are yet to hit the market.

By presenting an idea for a viable product likely to attract a huge amount of sales, you take a step towards building your business and scheduling your time in a better manner so as to maximize on both opportunities. A product with a distinct competitive advantage will ease you into the world of entrepreneurs.

It is just as important to set realistic goals that you can achieve as you set out to start a business. Setting goals is important because it will help you prioritize your time so that you can spend it equally in your employment position as well as running your prospective new business.

Realistic goals are measurable and achievable and it is important that you do the math before quitting your job. Finding the right balance involves dedicating enough time to the growth of your business but spending a reasonable amount of time at your daytime desk job.

You also need to prepare a road map of your business, and this is best done during the free time you can get in your daytime job. Find the appropriate course that your business should follow, from how you will open it and where to the point where you will quit your job and start running it fulltime.

A roadmap highlights important steps that must be followed in order to establish the business. These include activities like raising capital, seeking business advice and hiring staff members to run the operations of the business. A roadmap will give a clear direction of the actions you need to take.

After identifying your weaknesses, you should make sure to outsource those activities you do not prosper in because it can cause your business to collapse in the initial stages. If you do not have a sound understanding of different mathematical calculations, find somebody to assist you.

It is not appropriate to continue doing business in a field you are not specialist in and are not seeking advice. It is a big mistake to assume that you know and generalize your approach to handling different types of responsibilities. It is better to ask for help.

You should be on the prowl for constructive feedback from experienced entrepreneurs who are in a position to advice you. Spend some time speaking with people in your office as well as other business owners to gather as much information as possible about how best to run your business.

Seeking advice is a fundamental part of the business and it ensures that you stick o the right path. There are some upcoming entrepreneurs who find it embarrassing to ask for advice yet this is their avenue to success. Do not be afraid to seek a second opinion because it will shed light on the course of your business.

You should slowly start establishing a distinction between your daytime job and the business you want to start.

Separate time appropriately so that you maintain your normal working hours while setting aside extra time to handle the challenges of opening a new business.

It is not appropriate to mix the responsibilities of your current job with your emerging business. For instance, if your boss sends you uptown to handle a specific assignment, do not merge this time with the opportunity to look for more information for running your business because you will fail in both.

You must manage your time in the most effective way possible and prevent doing two things at the same time. Your boss is bound to notice that your concentration levels have dropped significantly and if they do find out that you are trying to start a business, you can easily be fired.

The best solution in this instance is to ensure that you separate the obligations of your current job completely until you are ready to quit. It is not wise to do both jobs concurrently as it will cause confusion and result in you making poor decisions that affect the future of your entrepreneurship.

Remember that it is only the success of your entrepreneurship that should prompt you to quit your daytime job. Do not be presumptuous and quit before the business has taken off because there is still a huge chance of failure. You will want a backup in case things do not go according to plan.

Most people quit their jobs too early before the business has picked and this often turns out to be a disastrous mistake. Of the many thousands of businesses opened every month in the United States, only a few achieve true success and are able to have an impact on their surrounding society.

You need to check the legal requirements of your current job position and whether you are able to start a business. You should consult a legal team so that they advice you whether you are breaching your contract in your place of work by venturing into entrepreneurship without severing your current contract.

Legal qualms are responsible for taking down more than thirty percent of new businesses that open in the United States every year. It is necessary to avoid any problems with your employer and confirming that it is okay for you to start a business while still contracted to another organization.

It might be useful for you to identify a suitable co-founder who can help you with the initial expenses and requirements for starting the business. Two is always better than one and finding a trusted friend will be a step towards ensuring you cover all the bases required for achieving success.

It usually is difficult to find somebody you can completely be transparent with, and so consider doing business with a member of the family. Their opinions, even though the ambition is yours will be invaluable because they will have an external view of the business.

While you are at work, you can entrust crucial operations necessary for setting up the entrepreneurship to a trusted friend. You can hire somebody you completely trust to handle the initial stages of the business because you will still need to report to work until your business has picked off.

This might not be the best of suggestions because should you find an untrustworthy person, you are likely to incur heavy losses. It is important for you to be there in the initial stages of your business, so create time to be visiting the business as you contemplate quitting your current job.

You need to separate your own personal finances with that of the upcoming business. Let there be a clear distinction between the two and do not let your personal life finance the emergence of your business. You should set aside capital for the business that you will not use for any personal reasons.

It is advisable to open an expense account that will specifically handle the expenditure associated with the new business. Do not mingle your personal finances into the running costs of the upcoming business because it will render you bankrupt before you know it.

Be sure to network within the specific industry that you want to start your business. Know as many people as possible so that you can ask for advice and assistance from relevant business figures who can actually point you in the right direction.

Networking will involve you making new friends and coming to an understanding with regard to the best way of setting up your business. You will also be able to establish connections in the market that allow you to find a suitable outlet for the products and services that your business specializes in.

Organize your time in an appropriate manner such that you spend daytime working on your office jobs while you spend nights following up on the progress of your business. Several entrepreneurs started out in this fashion and have ended up achieving much success.

You should divide up your time in an appropriate manner to ensure that you are never caught out. Do not make the mistake of trying to run your business while you are still in the office pursuing the objectives set for you by your employer. There has to be a clear difference between the two.

When running a new business, regardless of your employment status, think like a corporation. Imagine some of the actions that most companies would take to ensure the success of their operations. Now imagine yourself implementing such measures to guarantee the success of your own business.

When you think like a corporation, you develop a newfound respect for your business because you are able to visualize it bringing you immense success. Always pit your business with a larger comparable business already in the industry because it will act as guidance for you in making decisions.

You should be looking to invest in the cheapest marketing strategies to try and spread word of your new business. The success of a marketing strategy is not dependent on how much money you spend on an advertising campaign, but how well it has been executed.

It will be wise to handle the marketing efforts by yourself because it will give you an insight into the market and allow you to implement inventive ideas. These days, one of the cheapest ways of advertising is through the internet where you set up a social media account to provide information to prospective clients.

You should be familiar with effective ways of managing time because you should create time for your business in advance. Do not suspend important operations that require your concentration at that moment because it will disrupt the initial operations of the business and cause failure.

Always set aside time for handling your business affairs before actually getting into it to make sure that you are not intruding on anybody's time. Setting up the business to achieve success will require a lot of time management implementation to ensure that there is enough time to mitigate all risks facing the new business.

Only when your business has started running normally should you consider cutting back on your working hours progressively. Do not quit at once or create holidays for yourself all in the name of managing your business. Respect your current employment position first.

The best thing to do is slowly cut back the hours you spend in the office until the inevitable conversation you will share with your boss. Make sure that you are still contributing to your office but taking progressive measures to free yourself from the work. Do not quit suddenly as this might create a bad reputation for you.

Do not be discouraged if things do not go according to plan in the initial stages of the implementation of your business. Statistics suggest that over half the businesses that are opened in the United States alone every year do not prosper and end up collapsing.

While this is not good news, it is also a sign that not absolutely everything fails when the business is set up. It is still possible to achieve success with a few tweaks to your business operations and plans to guarantee that it can adapt to challenging situations and still yield a profit.

You also need to set aside time for resting and you abide by it because it is unhealthy to try and conduct two separate activities without taking a break. You should spend some alone time relaxing and contemplating your next move as this is the only way your mind will remain fresh and full of ideas.

Resting is a mandatory part of the emergence of any business because it gives you time to reflect on the decisions you have made. Just like a manuscript needs editing before publishing, entrepreneurship requires intelligent contemplation in a relaxed environment to ensure it can succeed.

Your best friend as you venture onto the path of entrepreneurship is the internet. This is an effective medium for conducting your research and finding out as much as possible about the available businesses and how to boost sales within your own enterprise.

The internet is responsible for revolutionizing business and you are able to collect lots of information online that will assist you in running your business. You can also access business courses online that will impart you specialist knowledge for running your entrepreneurship.

When launching yourself into the world of entrepreneurship, keep in mind that there are a lot of investment scams out there that have cost people lots of money. You should be wary of some of the schemes implemented by rogue individuals in a bid to con new business owners out of their money.

In order to avoid such scams as you set up your entrepreneurial business, always value a second opinion from somebody that you trust. Never agree to do business with somebody you o not know simply because they are giving you good investment options and are promising success.

It is also necessary to check the registration details of any business that you begin doing because you have to ascertain that it is legitimate. If you do business with companies that have not been registered, you are being fast tracked to lose your money because such companies are most likely run by conmen.

It is possible to check the registration details of any business by checking your local area directories. It is also possible to seek assistance online to find out the registration details of the business you are considering working with. Never do business with an organization that does not have valid registration details as it is likely a con.

You should never do business in a rushed manner even if you are eager to quit your full time job. This is why the prevalent advice is to wait for your business to achieve prosperity first before opting to quit your job. It is only after the business has picked that you can consider quitting your desk job.

Always take your time before making an investment decision because of most conmen like rushing potential victims so that they do not notice what they are trying to do. If you are attempting to launch a business with somebody who is pressuring you to act quickly, consider withdrawing from the venture.

Similarly, it is upon you to conduct extensive research into the market you want to venture into before making any investment decisions. In fact, research should be the activity at the forefront of your activities because you must find out everything about the businesses you want to liaise with.

When you begin your venture of entrepreneurship, it is important to collect as much information about the prospective business as you can. Never delve into something you are not familiar with unless you have conducted extensive research to understand what you are getting yourself into.

Remember that is it highly unwise to pay any advance fees when you are starting an entrepreneurial venture. If there are any expenses to be incurred, do research and recognize the fact that such expenditures will be made to a relevant authority. Never release the money to somebody you are not familiar with.

Since there are several businesses that open in the United States every year, it is also highly likely that there will be several conmen also looking to capitalize on the opportunities. Never pay any advance fees no matter how lucrative an investment seems to be because it is likely to be a con.

If you want to do business with an individual and they convince you by taking you to their offices, make sure you confirm later that it is indeed their official offices. Conmen are quite smart to convince prospective investors to come to dodgy offices in order to convince them to part with their money.

Most buildings are registered within a specific city council and you can take it upon yourself to find out more about the office ownership within. You need to ascertain that everything you are told by a potential investor is true before you even consider parting with your hard-earned cash.

If you want to invest in stocks and the forex markets, consider looking for legitimate stock brokers and traders who are registered in a specific stock exchange. Never fall for the trick of lucrative returns by investing in shady individuals because most of such ventures are cons.

Always follow the proper channels when venturing into the world of entrepreneurship because these channels have been set up for the protection of investors. There are several conmen who try to convince investors that they are financial traders and once they receive money, they disappear.

You should also consult extensively with a lawyer because they are capable of sharing relevant information with you that will point out fake investments. Lawyers have good connections and a fine understanding of the law and are likely to identify a fake investment opportunity when presented with one.

A lawyer will also give you critical legal advice that will be useful for setting up your business. Most entrepreneurs ignore legal advice, citing that it is expensive. However, this is the best guarantee of legitimacy that you will require in order to proceed with a specific investment.

There is a lot of controversy swirling around off-shore investments because they are seen as a perfect avenue for the rich in society to avoid paying taxes. It might be best for you to keep off these investments because they do not always guarantee lucrative returns.

Most off-shore investments are launched for a specific reason it is never to support other entrepreneurial ventures. Instead, off-shore investments are an excuse for money laundering and tax evasions. Despite the lucrative appeal of such investments, do not venture your entrepreneurial spirit in this direction.

One of the main characteristics of a fake investment opportunity is the promise of high returns and very low investment. The simple fact remains that most viable business opportunities require a reasonable amount of investment, time and legal documentation to support it.

Without these fundamental aspects of an investment, a potential entrepreneur is likely to fall into a con because they will be unable to identify the risks associated with such investments. Never agree to get into a business venture that barely requires anything to start but promises a massive return. This is a perfect excuse for conmen to swoop onto your finances and disappear.

You might also find yourself in a situation where you are being convinced by somebody to invest in a venture where they have inside information. This usually is a common con because most people want quick identifiable returns on their investment and insider information usually is the convincer.

However, most people who claim to have inside information usually lie. All they want to do is convince their customers that they can make quick money through a legitimate-looking scheme that has also brought them success. Never fall for this scam because insider information is usually not easy to come by.

When you find yourself being pressured to make an immediate purchase or investment, the likelihood is that you are being conned. For most legitimate business opportunities, investors are encouraged to take their time and think things over before making an investment decision.

However, in a situation where the potential investors are rushing you to close the deal even if you do not understand what is happening, you are likely being conned. Never agree to make a deal so quickly and always look to invest with patient investors so that you have all the time to conduct background checks and ascertain the viability of a business opportunity.

Always confirm the registration details of any venture you want to liaise with because you have to be certain that it is not a con. If you find that a business is not registered, the owners are probably trying to swindle money from you and disappear promptly.

It is sad that there are only a few investors who conduct thorough background checks to determine the legitimacy of different ventures. If you are unable to determine that a business has the right paperwork, licensing and registration, cu any investment ties you might have already established.

Most conmen do not like dealing in paperwork because they want to leave as little a paper trail as possible. You should be very wary of investing in such opportunities because it shows an element of illegitimacy about the businessmen. Paperwork is a vital part of any organization and you must always insist on seeing them.

You might discover that the people you are dealing with are very edgy and are constantly rushing you to complete a business deal. One of the important attributes of any entrepreneur is patience, and if the deal does not feel right, then simply walk away.

Entrepreneurs always value advice and they rarely act without asking several questions and conducting extensive research on the internet. Keep in mind the importance of educating and familiarizing yourself with an industry first even before considering putting cash into a venture.

There are many scams that exist out there, unfortunately, but with patience and proper research, it is possible to get past these hindrances. An entrepreneurial venture can only be built with precision and patience so make sure you do your homework thoroughly before making an investment.

When you finally quit your job, do so when the business is about to break-even and is posting impressive profits.

Conclusion

Thank you for making it through to the end of *Remote Work*, let's hope it was informative and able to provide you with all of the tools you need to achieve your goals whatever they may be.

The next step is to like us on social media. After reading this book, you should have comprehensive knowledge of the best approaches for starting a business and how to avoid common problems that result in business failure. It is necessary to understand the benefits of remote work, and a thorough description of this has been provided. After understanding the benefits, you should have the courage to venture into the field but be careful about quitting your job too soon. You should only consider leaving your job after you see a noticeable profit from your venture and its potential to sustain you over a long term period. Keep in mind that there are various approaches you can employ to get a viable remote job, and also take into consideration the valuable information you can get from job boards. Any successful entrepreneur values advice when it is given to them, so ensure that you are constantly attentive. In order to succeed in a remote job and eventually as an entrepreneur, team work is essential as it combines different good ideas to ensure the success of a venture. Lastly, avoid scams by being alert and patient because most conmen target eager investors who want to start doing business but are not knowledgeable enough to ensure its success.

Finally, if you found this book useful in any way, a review on Amazon is always appreciated!

Description

Remote work is gaining popularity progressively in the modern world as an increasing number of people are turning to business from their employment positions. In the United States alone, millions of small businesses open each year, but there is a varying rate of success for all of them. The most successful businesses follow strict business principles and stick to a code of operating in such a manner as never to venture beyond their means. There are numerous remote jobs available in the world, in fact, they are limitless. It is almost impossible to keep track of the different opportunities that one can venture in, and it explains why so many people are willing to quit their full time jobs. The astounding rate at which businesses are opening across the United States and the rest of the world is particularly encouraging for entrepreneurs. It is driving a large number of people to search for capital to start their own businesses, as well. However, despite all the positive aspects of entrepreneurship, the creation of opportunities has also led to the emergence of a large number of conmen looking to capitalize on the growing sector. Conducting prior research before making an investment is as important as ever.

- The book provides practical investment advice for those looking to start an entrepreneurial career.

- The book provides excellent comparisons between remote work and desk office jobs to determine the most suitable in the present time.

- There is a list of different websites as well as different remote jobs that individuals can engage in and quit their normal desk jobs.

- There is also advice on the best approaches for starting entrepreneurship with the information provided on the steps to follow.

- There is also personalized information on the best approaches for those looking for remote jobs to ensure that they find what they are looking for.

www.ingramcontent.com/pod-product-compliance
Lightning Source LLC
Chambersburg PA
CBHW021814170526
45157CB00007B/2580